SERIES ON
ECONOMIC DEVELOPMENT
AND GROWTH VOL. 8

INSTITUTIONAL CHANGE
AND THE DEVELOPMENT
OF INDUSTRIAL CLUSTERS
IN CHINA
CASE STUDIES FROM THE TEXTILE
AND CLOTHING INDUSTRY

Series on Economic Development and Growth (ISSN: 1793-3668)

SERIES ON
ECONOMIC DEVELOPMENT
        AND GROWTH VOL. 8

INSTITUTIONAL CHANGE AND THE DEVELOPMENT OF INDUSTRIAL CLUSTERS IN CHINA

CASE STUDIES FROM THE TEXTILE AND CLOTHING INDUSTRY

Jinmin Wang

Nottingham Trent University, UK

 World Scientific

NEW JERSEY · LONDON · SINGAPORE · BEIJING · SHANGHAI · HONG KONG · TAIPEI · CHENNAI

Published by

World Scientific Publishing Co. Pte. Ltd.
5 Toh Tuck Link, Singapore 596224
USA office: 27 Warren Street, Suite 401-402, Hackensack, NJ 07601
UK office: 57 Shelton Street, Covent Garden, London WC2H 9HE

Library of Congress Cataloging-in-Publication Data
Wang, Jinmin.
    Institutional change and the development of industrial clusters in China : case studies from the textile and clothing industry / by Jinmin Wang (Nottingham Trent University, UK).
        pages cm. -- (Series on economic development and growth, ISSN 1793-3668 ; vol. 8)
        Includes bibliographical references and index.
        ISBN 978-9814289047
        1. Industrial clusters--China--Case studies. 2. Textile industry--China--Case studies.
3. Clothing industry--China--Case studies. 4. Organizational change--China--Case studies.
I. Title.
        HC430.D5W36 2014
        338.8'7--dc23
                                                                    2013002858

British Library Cataloguing-in-Publication Data
A catalogue record for this book is available from the British Library.

In-house Editors: Sandhya Venkatesh/Dipasri Sardar

Typeset by Stallion Press
E-mail: enquiries@stallionpress.com

Printed in Singapore

CONTENTS

PREFACE

I was born and grew up in Yiwu County, Zhejiang province, East China before leaving for the study at Hangzhou University in 1989, which is part of Zhejiang University now. In my childhood, I remembered clearly that there were only two main streets in Choucheng Town, where Yiwu County Municipal Government was located. But now the two narrow streets have become part of the flourishing downtown area. Yiwu City has been developed into one of the leading county-level commercial cities in China with the world's largest commodity trading market. Each time when I go back to my hometown, I am amazed at its rapid urbanization and economic development in the past three decades. I always wonder how a small county-level city without rich natural resources and heavy state investment can transform itself into a modern international city within such a short time.

However, it is not the single successful story of regional development in Zhejiang Province. On the train to Ningbo City in my pilot study in 2005, I observed the China Textile City in Shaoxing County for the first time, which had grown up in the neighborhood of a large scale agglomeration of small- and medium-sized textile and clothing firms, textile machinery and equipment agents on the way. When I was shown around Youngor International Garments City in Ningbo City, I was very impressed by the modern office building and a series of large workshops involved in weaving, dyeing, clothing-making and distribution. The employees were operating the first-class modern specialist equipment for design, slope-making, feeding and auto-cutting made in France, all kinds of ready-made clothes hanging systems and specialized finishing and binding machines made in Germany, and post-weaving trimmers made in Italy. In Yinzhou District where Youngor Group is located, I observed the high agglomeration of small and medium-sized as well as large clothing firms, clothing accessory firms, universities, and textile and clothing test centers. At the end of my pilot study, I decided to study the development model of textile and clothing clusters in Zhejiang Province, which can partly explain how China has become the world's largest producer and exporter of textiles and clothing products in the past decades.

When I started my research project in 2005, there was a new round of privatization in the Chinese economy. Management Buy-Out (MBO) was used as the principal means of privatizing some State-Owned Enterprises (SOEs). As the reform deepened, there were widespread debates on the use of MBO as a means of privatizing SOEs both in the academic circle and within the society at large. Curious about privatization, institutional reform and regional development in China, scholars were concerned to discover whether there were any other better and more just alternatives to the use of MBOs in the privatization process. At the same time, the scholars became increasingly drawn to the study of the rapid development of the private sector in China more generally.

In its reform from a centrally planned to a market economy over the past three decades, China has developed from a rural agricultural society to a modern industrial one. In the 1980s and 1990s, the dynamism of China's economic growth came mainly from the collectively owned township and village enterprises, but since the late 1990s, the private enterprise has become an increasingly important driving force. In 2005, the Chinese government opened more sectors to private investors to include infrastructure construction, financial services and even the defence industry, previously monopolized by state firms, enabling the private sector to exert greater influence on economic transition in China. As a result, private enterprises participated in the restructuring of SOEs and entered previously monopolized sectors in this new phase of privatization.

The synthetic fiber industry is in the middle of an industrial chain with the oil industry upstream and the textile industry downstream. In China, the oil industry is still a state monopoly. In recent years, the pace of private firms entering the petrochemical industry and moving upstream has accelerated with the rapid development of the textile industry and the considerable increase of textile exports to the world market after China's entry into the WTO at the end of 2001. Private enterprises have dominated downstream of the synthetic fiber industry but upstream the industry is still controlled by the state-owned oil companies. However, in order to meet fierce domestic and international competitions, the private textile enterprises had to adopt the vertical integration strategy and move towards the upstream of industrial chain. Some of them initiated a program of producing polyester first and then producing the upstream material such as terephthalic acid (PTA). The purpose of this study was to explore the relationship between institutional change and economic development in contemporary China; to identify the likely institutional, social and political implications of expanding the private sector there; specifically, to examine how the government–business relationship evolve in the process of formation, development and internationalization of textile and clothing clusters in rural China.

My working experience at School of Economics and School of Public Administration, Zhejiang University has contributed to my understanding and critical analysis of private economy and regional development in Zhejiang Province. I am very happy that the book can be published because it records some of the unique elements of regional development in rural China. As an overseas scholar, I am very proud of the achievement Zhejiangnese have made in the past three decades!

Jinmin Wang
Nottingham, the United Kingdom

ACKNOWLEDGMENT

I am grateful to a large number of people and organizations, without whose help, this book could not have been completed.

In the United Kingdom, I want to extend my sincere gratitude to Professor Shujie Yao, Head of School of Contemporary Chinese Studies, the University of Nottingham, who encouraged me to publish the book. Professor Richard Sanders, Professor Peter Lawrence and Professor Nada Kakabadse at the University of Northampton granted me enormous encouragement and academic guidance with their rich knowledge and professional expertise in carrying out the research project and completing the study.

In China, I am indebted to countless numbers of scholars, local government officials, managers and employees of SMEs in Zhejiang Province, who warmly and patiently answered my questions in my fieldwork. My sincere thanks go to Professor Jinchuan Shi and Professor Xianguo Yao at Zhejiang University for their insightful guidance and great help with the research.

In addition, I want to thank Ms Dipasri Sardar, editor at Academic Consulting and Editorial Services (ACES) Pvt Ltd in India and Ms Sandhya Venkatesh, senior editor at World Scientific Press in Singapore for their marvelous support in editing and publishing the book.

Finally, I can hardly express the debt of gratitude I owe to my family for their love and support in writing the book. My heartfelt gratitude goes to my father, Guanwen Wang, my mother, Lianxiang Jiang, my wife, Dan Chen and my dearest daughters, Zixin Wang and Lilian Chen. This book is dedicated to them.

ABOUT THE AUTHOR

Dr Jinmin Wang is Lecturer at School of Contemporary Chinese Studies, the University of Nottingham, the United Kingdom. He previously worked at Zhejiang University, East China and Nottingham Trent University, the United Kingdom. Jinmin has special research interests in regional development and international business management in contemporary China. He has undertaken a wide range of research projects including the role of specialized markets in the collective internationalization process of SMEs in rural China, the business model innovation of Norwegian and Spanish multinational companies in China. He has had consultancy experiences with some of the major international organizations such as the South Centre and the United Nations Economic and Social Commission for Asia and the Pacific (ESCAP).

LIST OF TABLES

LIST OF FIGURES

1

INTRODUCTION

1.1. The Development of Private Economy in China's Post-Reform

The Third Plenum of the Chinese Communist Party's (CCP) 11th Central Committee in December 1978 initiated the market-oriented reforms and the adoption of open-door policy in China. The introduction of the household responsibility system improved farmers' income and created a labor surplus. A set of State Council regulations on the urban, non-agricultural individual economy was issued in July 1981, which defined a new business category — single industrial and commercial proprietor. As a result, the private economic sector started to develop again. In 1983, a series of central and local regulations for the licensing and control of individual businesses, taxation, product quality and hygiene, and free markets were introduced in China. The development of private business was affected by the following "market rectification" drives. In June 1988, the State Council issued the *Tentative Stipulations on Private Enterprises*, where private enterprises were defined as for-profit organizations that are owned by individuals and employ more than eight people (Garnaut *et al.*, 2012). The ownership of private enterprises range from sole proprietorship, partnerships, limited liability companies to shareholding cooperatives. Different requirements were set for registered capital and numbers of shareholders with different forms of private ownership (ADB, 2003).

Deng Xiaoping's southern tour in September 1992 accelerated China's transition to the rapid development of a socialist market-oriented economy. The 14th Party Congress witnessed ideological breakthrough and the establishment of a major socialist market economy was listed on the reform agenda of the national economy. The state-owned enterprises (SOEs) started to transform the ownership and undertake the reform of clarification of property rights. The Third Plenary Session of the 14th Party Congress in November 1993 decided to divest small SOEs from state control. The policy of "keeping the large and letting the small go" was carried out in 1995. The ownership structure of SOEs was diversified through a range of processes including contracting, leasing, establishing an employee-held company or cooperative, even outright privatization. In March 1999, the National People's Congress passed an amendment to the constitution to recognize the status of the private sector. The legitimacy of private property rights was gradually accepted ideologically, politically and constitutionally (Garnaut *et al.*, 2012).

The definition of the private sector has been still vague and fuzzy in terms of enterprise types in China. The term "non-state" has been more widely used as a broader category than "private" (ADB, 2003). Nonetheless, the presence of the private sector has become increasingly significant in the Chinese economy (see Table 1.1). For the commercial business sector, the percentage of value added by private firms was esti-mated at 63% in 2003, up from about 54% in 1998. The private share of the non-farm business sector moved ahead of the public share for the first time between 1998 and 2003, with its share of output rising from 43% in 1998 to 57% in 2003. About one-third of the increase in the size of the private sector was reflected in a decline in the number and output of collectives, with the remaining two-thirds reflected in closure and divest-ment of solely state-owned firms. The state-owned share of value added fell from 58% in 1998 to 43% in 2003 with about half of this being the result of an injection of minority stakes from the private sector. In the economy as a whole, the private share of GDP rose from 50% of value added in 1998 to 59% in 2003 (OECD, 2005).

In 2005, the Chinese government opened more sectors to private inves-tors to include infrastructure construction, financial services and even the defense industry, previously monopolized by the state firms, enabling the private sector to exert greater influence on economic transition in China. As a result, private enterprises participated in the restructuring of SOEs and entered previously monopolized sectors in this new phase of privati-zation. With the increasing significance of private enterprises in the

Table 1.1. The private sector outpaces the public sector (percent of value added by firm ownership).

	1998	1999	2000	2001	2002	2003
Non-farm business sector						
Private sector	43.0	45.3	47.7	51.8	54.6	57.1
Public sector	57.0	54.7	52.3	48.2	45.4	42.9
State-controlled	40.5	40.1	39.6	37.1	35.2	34.1
Collective	16.5	14.7	12.7	11.2	10.1	8.8
Total (79% of GDP)	100.0	100.0	100.0	100.0	100.0	100.0
Business sector						
Private sector	53.5	54.9	56.3	59.4	61.5	63.3
Public sector	46.5	45.1	43.7	40.6	38.5	36.7
State-controlled	33.1	33.0	33.1	31.2	29.9	29.2
Collective	13.4	12.1	10.6	9.4	8.6	7.5
Total (94% of GDP)	100.0	100.0	100.0	100.0	100.0	100.0
Economy-wide						
Private sector	50.4	51.5	52.8	55.5	57.4	59.2
Public sector	49.6	48.5	47.2	44.5	42.6	40.8
State-controlled	36.9	37.1	37.3	35.7	34.6	33.7
Collective	12.7	11.3	10.0	8.8	8.0	7.1
Total (100% of GDP)	100.0	100.0	100.0	100.0	100.0	100.0

Source: OECD (2005, p. 81).

national economy, 1,554 entrepreneurs in the private sector joined the CCP and about 32.2% entrepreneurs of private firms were party members in 2006 (Gao, 2007).

1.2. The Emergence of Industrial Clusters in China

The formation and growth of industrial clusters has taken place within the context of ownership reform of SOEs and the rapid development of the private economy along the coastal provinces in China. The industrial clusters have played an important role in stimulating the regional development and strengthening the local–global linkage. Some of them have exhibited similar features to those in Italy (Wang, 2011).

Many industrial clusters composed of small- and medium-sized enterprises (SMEs) were first established in the towns and cities in the coastal region, particularly the Pearl River Delta and the Yangtze River Delta along the process of rural industrialization. Different paths of economic growth have emerged known as "the Pearl River Delta Model" (Guangdong province, South China), "the South Jiangsu Model" (Jiangsu province, East China), "the Wenzhou Model" (Zhejiang province, East China) and "the Yiwu Model" (Zhejiang province, East China), stimulating the regional economic development.

The formation of the "Pearl River Delta Model" was attributed to the open-door policy of 1978. In the mid-1980s, the special economic zones in the Pearl River Delta were established and the Township and Village Enterprises (TVEs) in the region had very high outward dependency. With the transformation of their role as processors for joint ventures and solely foreign-funded enterprises, both foreign capital and advanced management practices were introduced to China (Yang, 2007).

"The Wenzhou model" emerged in the 1980s. Wenzhou is a prefecture-level municipality in the southeast corner of coastal Zhejiang province with a population of over six million, covering 11,800 square kilometers including two municipal districts, one inland city and eight rural counties. It is a mountainous area with limited cultivated farm land and poor transportation infrastructure. The initial foundation for industrial development was weak. Rural industrialization in Wenzhou was achieved mainly through thousands of family workshops closely linked to the "Commodity trading markets". "Small commodities, big markets" is often used to describe the rapid economic growth in Zhejiang province. The commodities used to be mainly daily necessities with small-scale production, limited technology content and lower cost of transport. The formation of industrial clusters in Wenzhou and even the whole Zhejiang province was demonstrated as hundreds of family workshops engaged in the same industry and agglomerated in neighboring villages or towns (Shi *et al.*, 2002; Wei *et al.*, 2007).

The "South Jiangsu Model" emphasized greater enterprise autonomy, but it was based on the predominance of small SOEs and local TVEs that did not follow the radical privatization path of the Wenzhou model. Jiangsu Province adopted a policy to encourage the formation of collective shareholding enterprises in 1995, which required coordination with local governments at a time when disengagement and general privatization was already being propagated in Zhejiang. From 1999 onwards, local governments were required to reduce their control over or shares in collective enterprises and small SOEs by 2002. The industrial clusters in the southern part of Jiangsu province concentrated on labor-intensive, capital-intensive and technology-intensive industries, including synthetic fibers, construction materials, information technology (IT) and the manufacturing of heavy machinery equipment (Wang and Shi, 2006; Wei *et al.*, 2009).

The bottom-up nature of rural industrialization in Zhejiang province resembles industrial clustering in northern Italy (Wang, 2001; Lu and Ganne, 2009). Firstly, the industrial clusters of both Zhejiang and Italy concentrate on light industries such as textiles including socks, clothes and ties. Secondly, although large firms are present in both contexts and are integral to cluster dynamics (Guerrieri and Pietrobelli, 2001; Wang *et al.*, 2007), SMEs are the predominant element both in the Zhejiang province and Italian clusters. In both clusters, these firms are characterized by substantial flexibility and innovativeness (Piore and Sabel, 1984; Becattini, 1990; Guerrieri and Iammarino, 2001; Marukawa, 2009). Thirdly, the industrial clusters in Zhejiang province exhibit the same awareness of the need for innovation, the same preference for initiating family-based businesses and the same spirit for taking risks as those in Italy (Chen, 2000; Wang and Shi, 2006). Moreover, in both countries, the local–global linkages between industrial clusters and international markets have been strengthened through the formation of strategic alliances with foreign firms for technology transfer (Wang, 2001; Pietrobelli, 2004; Gambarotto and Solari, 2005).

Although the industrial clusters in Zhejiang province, East China, match the Italian model to some extent, they have their own unique trajectory of growth and development. The most prominent and distinctive feature of cluster development in Zhejiang province, in contrast to cluster development in Italy, has been the role of local government in deliberately and purposively establishing and developing large-scale "Commodity trading markets", which have contributed to the linkage with the huge domestic market and overseas business expansion. The research in the Ningbo clothing cluster, the Shaoxing synthetic fiber cluster and the Yiwu socks cluster, all in Zhejiang Province, shows that the local government plays an important role in the formation, development and upgrading of industrial clusters.

1.3. Institutional Change and the Development of Industrial Clusters

The changes of the past three decades outlined above have attracted considerable research both within China and the rest of the world. This book seeks to contribute to this research, albeit by means of a selective emphasis. Thus, the main objective of this book is to explore the relationship between the complicated interactive process of institutional change and the development of industrial clusters in China. It focuses on how institutional change has led to the formation and development of industrial clusters. Industrial clusters play an important part in regional development in China because it can generate collective efficiency through economic agglomeration, eventually leading to regional innovation and competitive advantage (Bellandi and Lombardi, 2012).

This research has been carried out with institution theory, giving weight to institutional change through multiple case studies of textile and clothing clusters in Zhejiang province, East China. The institutional approach provides one broad framework to study the process of economic transition in general, which is a complex economic and social phenomenon. The micro case studies, which are effective in illustrating the interaction between institutional change and industrial development, have shown that the evolution of political and economic institutions determine the economic performance of transitional economies eventually because they create an incentive structure of the whole society. The evolution of the institutional matrix has had great impact on the formation and growth of industrial clusters in the course of regional development in rural China in transition.

North (1981, pp. 201–202) defined institutions as "a set of rules, compliance procedures, and moral and ethical behavioral norms designed to constrain the behavior of individuals in the interest of maximizing the wealth or utility of principals". Institutions are routines, habits and social rules affecting the interaction among individuals, including political, economic and social institutions. There are formal institutions such as constitutions, laws, bills of rights, courts, regulations and standards, which form legal and political frameworks for social interactions. In addition, there are informal institutions, such as cultural norms, conventions, codes of conduct, norms of behavior, traditions, habits, attitudes and generally accepted, but informal procedures for governing social interactions (North, 1990).

Institutional changes have played a critical role in shaping the opportunities of actors and in allowing supporting certain types of behavior, while discouraging others (Beckert, 2010). In this book, institution means "a system of socially produced regularities that shape, and are in turn shaped by, individual behaviors" (Kuran, 2010, p. 6).

Institutions possess three basic functions including the reduction of uncertainity, management of cooperation and conflicts, and provision of incentives that influence behavior in human interaction (Edquist and Johnson, 1997). According to Scott (2002, pp. 170–174), "the use of institutional logics, actors and governance structures to examine institutional structures and processes in organizational fields. Institutional logics refer to belief systems and associated practices that are operative in a field. They combine both culture-cognitive and normative elements. Institutional actors, both individual and collective, create, embody and enact the logics of the field. Governance structures operate (e.g., nation-state structures), affecting the field's structure and activities. Such structures typically combine normative and regulative elements".

As suggested above, the Chinese government has withdrawn significantly from many parts of the economy although the core public utility and resource-based industries remain in public hands. In the remaining non-core industries that represent more than two-thirds of industrial output, state firms only produce about one-quarter of value added and are subject to competitive forces. Restructuring in the industrial sector has been most rapid, representing 57% of non-farm business sector value added in 2003. In the eastern coastal region (especially Zhejiang, Guangdong and Jiangsu provinces), the share of industrial value added from the private sector is 63% against only 32% in other regions. In manufacturing, foreign enterprise growth was in the electronics and telecommunication equipment sector while they were much less active than domestic enterprises in sectors such as textiles and smelting steel

(OECD, 2005). However, the further reform of SOEs makes more room for the expansion of private sector. This does not simply mean the complete state withdrawal and allows the private sector to take over. The general picture in China shows that the rapid growth of private firms in China has been accompanied by frequent changes in ownership, new organizational forms and the structure of property rights.

The growth of private firms has been closely linked to the restructuring of SOEs in the course of cluster development in China. The effective SOE reform has partly depended on the success in carrying out the transition tasks at the critical stage of the growth of private enterprises. When industrial clusters in China are in the process of rapid development and constant upgrading, a lot of clustered firms have inevitably participated in the further restructuring of SOEs or formed alliances with SOEs and foreign-funded enterprises as they pursue the strategy of diversification. Some clustered firms have become listed on the stock exchanges by buying a SOE shell so as to improve their financing capability through the capital market.

The report of the 17th national congress of the communist party of China by President Hu Jintao in October 2007 emphasized the significance of upholding and improving the basic economic system in which public ownership is dominant and different economic sectors develop side by side, unwaveringly consolidating and developing the public sector of the economy, unswervingly encouraging, supporting and guiding the development of the non-public sector, ensuring equal protection of property rights, and creating a new situation in which all economic sectors compete on an equal footing and reinforcing each other. The reform of collectively-owned enterprises was pressed ahead with and various forms of collective and cooperative economic operations will be developed. The development of individually-owned businesses and private companies as well as SMEs were promoted with equitable market access, a better financing environment and less institutional barriers. The central government continued to develop the economic sector with mixed ownership (Hu, 2007).

The local government established many "Commodity trading markets" in the coastal provinces in the 1980s. They were spread to other parts of China throughout the 1990s. The emergence and growth of many industrial clusters have been closely related to the "Commodity trading markets". They are closely inter-related and inter-dependent. Many "Commodity trading markets" have promoted the growth of industrial clusters while many industrial clusters have, in turn, enlarged the scope and scale of the specialized wholesale markets. With the effective management and administration of the local government, some "Commodity trading markets" have achieved great success and even internationalized in the era of globalization, leading to the upgrading of relevant clusters.

"There is no one best model for organizing an industrial district or cluster. A diversity of institutional arrangements is possible and each has proved successful in different circumstances" (Carlo, 2004, p. 185). This book is designed to offer a better understanding of the interplay between institutional change and the rapid development of industrial clusters in China in general, using the textile and clothing clusters in Zhejiang province as case studies.

1.4. State, Institutional Change and Economic Development

China's economic reform has been characterized by non-predictive gradualism (Naughton, 2007). Although the market-oriented reform has been deepened since the beginning of 21st century, China is still unique in the continuity of political power in the hands of CCP alongside the rapid changing of economic organization. Institutional change in China has frequently been a creative process. When China uses the cluster approach to achieve similar goals as other developing and developed countries all over the world, it is important to take its typical transitional context into account. The book intends to explore the unique institutional factors that have distinguished SME industrial clusters in China and those in other transitional economies and developed countries. So far, the academic researches on industrial clusters in China has attached much importance to the design and implementation of cluster policies, the innovation and upgrading of industrial clusters and the integration of industrial clusters into the global value chains (GVC). This book, however, concentrates primarily on how institutional change contributes to the development of textile and clothing clusters in rural China in transition in the first place.

There is diversity in economic regimes in the Chinese economy (see Table 1.2). The different sets of institutions can be identified by three forms

Table 1.2.   The diversity of economic regimes in China.

Key features	Neo-classical state	Developmental state	Corporatist state
Economic growth	Market-oriented economy	State planning and regulating the economy through controlling the resources	State as "partner"
Organizational change	Tolerance of new organizational forms	Sector-specific organizational forms	Fuzzy organizational choice
Property rights regime	Domination by the private ownership	Public–private hybrid ownership	Collective consensus
R&D	Market-driven innovation	Domination by the state	Network-driven
Economic performance	Competition	State-defined constraint	Lobbying, bargaining and negotiation

Sources: Schmitter (1974), Wade (1990), and Krug and Hendrischke (2008).

in the development of industrial clusters: (i) the neo-classical state in which economic activities are mainly regulated by market forces; (ii) the developmental state in which the government plays a strategic role in taming domestic and international market forces and harnessing them to national ends; and (iii) the corporatist state is defined as a system of interest representation in which the constituent units are organized into a limited number of singular, compulsory, non-competitive, hierarchically ordered and functionally differentiated categories, recognized or licensed by the state and granted a deliberate representational monopoly within their respective categories in exchange for observing certain controls on their selection of leaders and articulation of demands and supports (Schmitter, 1974).

In the past decades, the neo-classical paradigm has prevailed and been pursued widely by the international organizations including the World Bank, the International Monetary Fund (IMF) and the World Trade Organization (WTO). According to the paradigm, the most successful emerging economies in the world were brought about through an outward-oriented model stimulated by market incentives and powerful private sectors. The World Bank even proposed a "market-friendly" approach for the role of government, in which the state acts only in the case of market failure. In this paradigm, the government plays only a passive role in the development process and the market mechanism distorts with government intervention (World Bank, 1993).

In contrast, the developmental state paradigm argues that the state has played a strategic role through harnessing domestic and international market forces to national ends in East Asian economic development (Amsden, 1989; Evans, 1995, Hsu, 2004, 2010). Industrialization rather than comparative advantage has contributed to economic growth. The state controls the operations of the market in the process of industrialization. Evans (1995) indicates that states vary in the way they are organized and tied to the society and, therefore, play different roles such as custodians, demiurge, midwifery and husbandry in different countries after conducting a comparative study of hi-tech industries in South Korea, Brazil and India. "It is an autonomy embedded in a concrete set of social ties that bind the state to society and provide institutionalized channels for the continual negotiation and renegotiation of goals and policies" (Evans, 1995, p. 50).

The paradigm of state corporatism shares the authority with social groups. The cooperation between the state and social groups is of great significance to economic development. The business relations depend on lobbying, bargaining and negotiating within the corporate sector. The paradigm indicates that networks can serve as the dominant organizing form of production and exchange. Whether network-supported sectors develop into state-guaranteed (local) monopolies depends on the competition home and abroad as well as the interaction among these networks and the political leadership. The property rights are mainly collective or fuzzy. The individual interests are usually represented by one collective agent. The Research and Development (R&D) sector, which is mainly network-driven, depends on the cooperation and support of social groups that can mobilize the necessary resources. The individual property rights under the paradigm of state corporatism are weak and the performance of firms depends on the collective efficiency of networks (Schmitter, 1974; Krug and Hendrischke, 2008). Oi (1999) extended the paradigm to "local state corporatism" to describe the rural development in China in the 1990s. She described the Chinese cases as a subcategory of state corporatism, which was mainly constituted and coordinated by the local government (counties, townships and villages) instead of the central government. In the 1990s, local state corporatism emerged as the local government moved from simpler and more cadre-centered forms of governance to a mixed model appropriate to a vastly larger industrial economy consisting of both private and collective enterprises.

The research has shown that the above three types of economic regimes have been established by different hierarchies of government. They co-exist and have undergone the dynamic change, which have led to the rapid development of textile and clothing clusters in China. The reality in China, as indicated through case studies of this book, will reveal that the nature of the local state–business relationship is taking up a new shape even though it is still vague and hybrid. The transitional path of China is so unusual that it casts doubt on much of the conventional thinking on fundamental issues concerning system changes and the process of reform (Chow, 1997). Much research has been done using data from China to test existing theories, but studying China's experience in globalization is even more useful for generating new theories, especially in the area of institutional change.

1.5. Plan of the Book

The previous discussions outline the main research objectives, questions and approach of this book. The following chapters deal with the issues of those concerns and offer a framework for understanding the complicated interactive process of institutional change and the development of textile and clothing clusters in China in transition.

Chapter 2 conducts a literature review on the concept and typology of industrial clusters, competitive advantage and industrial clusters, institutional change under economic reform in transitional China.

Chapter 3 discusses the development of textile and clothing industry in China since the adoption of open-door policy in 1978. It is followed by an analysis of the evolution of global textile and clothing trade regime, and its impacts on the development of textile and clothing clusters in China.

Chapter 4 gives an overview of institutional change and the development of industrial clusters in Zhejiang Province. The role of informal and formal institutions in the formation and development of industrial clusters is explored here.

Chapters 5 to 7 present evidence of institutional change and development of three well-known textile and clothing clusters in Zhejiang province, namely, Ningbo clothing cluster, Shaoxing textile cluster and Yiwu socks cluster.

Chapter 8 concludes with answers to the research questions on the basis of the evidence in the previous chapters. Specifically, it argues that the unique institutional factors leading to the rapid development of industrial clusters in China include institutional entrepreneurship and commodity trading market. The development and upgrading of textile and clothing clusters in China have witnessed the extraordinary institutional change through the co-evolution between the public sector and the private sector. It is an interactive and dynamic process coupled with the ownership change influenced by ideology and political factors.

2

INSTITUTIONS, INDUSTRIAL CLUSTERS AND REGIONAL DEVELOPMENT

2.1. Introduction

Industrial clusters play an important role in promoting economic growth and regional development both in developed and developing countries (Cooke and Morgan, 1998; Porter, 1998; Perry, 2005; Shahid *et al.*, 2008; Monga, 2011). The competitive advantage of a nation not only relies on large firms, but also on SMEs. With more and more fierce global competition, SMEs need to establish all kinds of linkages to transmit information and creative ideas and improve their competitive advantage (Karaev *et al.*, 2007). International organizations such as the World Bank the United Nations Industrial Development Organization have been encouraging developing countries to implement the cluster strategy to promote regional industrial development (UNIDO, 2000; Yutaka, 2011; Tetsushi *et al.*, 2012). Since the mid-1990s, both developing and developed countries have implemented public policies to promote the development of regional industrial clusters and integrate local production systems within the GVC (Humphrey and Humphrey, 2002; Giuliani *et al.*, 2005a, 2005b). The creation of industrial clusters has been regarded as an important strategy to improve the competitive advantage of a nation and to cope with the fierce global economic competition.

2.2. Concepts and Types of Industrial Clusters

Marshall (1891) is often cited as the first economist to recognize that the location and proximity of firms can lead to an improvement in their productivity and business. He listed three fundamental advantages for clustered firms in the form of externalities: A pooled market for skilled workers with industry-specific competencies that prevent labor shortage, the availability of non-tradable and intermediate inputs provided by local suppliers and the easy transmission of new ideas that allows more efficient production functions through technical, organizational and production improvements. Marshall identified the possible static and dynamic effects of spatial agglomeration of economic activities, enhancing the efficiency and the growth of firms located in an industrial cluster. Developing along the path set by the Marshallian tradition at the end of the 1970s, a group of Italian scholars introduced a new definition of industrial cluster, as "a socio-territorial entity which is characterized by the active presence of both a community of people and a population of firms in one naturally and historically bounded area (Becattini, 1990, p. 38)." This definition attaches more importance to socio-political factors, links between suppliers and clients and the impact of the community on enhancing the performance of firms within industrial clusters. According to Porter (2000), clusters are groups of companies and institutions co-located in a specific geographic region and linked by interdependencies in providing a related group of products and/or services. That is, industrial clusters not only include a series of relevant industries and entities such as specialized input suppliers, but also extend to clients in the lower stream and complementary products such as relevant know-how and technology in the upper stream.

Up to now, the definition of industrial clusters varies greatly in academic circles. Different subjects have created their respective terminology on the phenomenon. For example, "local production systems" and "industrial districts" are commonly used in economic geography. In fact, various definitions convey the same economic phenomenon of many firms agglomerating within one location, but they have different emphases. For example, Porter's definition of "industrial clusters" stresses competitiveness while the definition of "new industrial district" in economic geography attaches more importance to the social and cultural factors (Zhu, 2003). However, some scholars argue that industrial cluster is a chaotic concept because it lacks clear boundaries in terms of geographical scale and internal social-economic dynamics (Martin and Sunley, 2003).

Industrial clusters differ in geographical location, development stages and industrial types. Garofoli (1991) categorizes the industrial clusters in

Italy into specialized production areas, local production system and system areas by taking into account factors such as entrepreneurship, production structure, enterprise size, inter-firm relationships, local labor market, innovation sources, social structure and local institutions. The inter-firm cooperation in the specialized production area is weak. The SMEs, which are engaged in the same industry, have to compete for the same market segment. In the local production system, the SMEs also confront constant horizontal competition. However, the social and cultural traditions contribute to knowledge diffusion and industrial upgrading in the region. System areas are a more advanced type of industrial agglomeration than specialized production areas and local production system. There is a clear division of labor in the same sector or related sectors among the SMEs in the region. The production equipments may also be manufactured and supplied locally (Guerrieri and Pietrobelli, 2001).

Markusen (1996a) identified three new types of industrial districts including hub-and-spoke district, the satellite industrial platform and the state-anchored industrial district in addition to Marshallian industrial districts (Table 2.1). A hub-and-spoke district revolves around one or several leading firms in one or several industries which act as hubs to the regional economy, with suppliers and related activities spread around them like the spokes of a wheel. A satellite industrial platform consists of a congregation of branch facilities of externally based multi-plant firms that are induced by the policies of national or local governments to stimulate the regional development. The key investment decisions are made out of the industrial district (ID). The tenants of satellite platform must be more or less spatially independent from upstream or downstream operations as well as from the agglomeration of other competitors and suppliers in the same area. There tend to be minimal collaboration among platform firms, which are often engaged in different activities and industries. The constraints on the development of this type of industrial district include the shortage of local resources such as finance, technical expertise, business services and industry-specific trade associations that may provide shared resources and services. In the state-anchored district, a public or non-profit entity, such as a university, a military base, a defence plant, or the government research complexes, acts as a key anchor tenant in the district. The industrial parks and science parks may fall within this category. They

Table 2.1.   Types and features of new industrial districts.

Types	Features
Marshallian industrial districts	• Business structure dominated by small, locally-owned firms. • Scale economies relatively low. • Substantial intradistrict trade among buyers and suppliers. • Key investment decisions made locally. • Long-term contracts and commitments between local buyers and suppliers. • Low degrees of cooperation or linkage with firms external to the district. • Labor market internal to the district, highly flexible. • Workers committed to district, rather than to firms. • High rates of labor in-migration, lower levels of out-migration. • Evolution of unique local cultural identity, bonds. • Specialized sources of finance, technical expertise, business services available in district outside of firms. • Existence of "patient capital" within district. • Turmoil, but good long-term prospects for growth and employment.
Italianate variant	In addition to the above: • High incidence of exchanges of personnel between customers and suppliers. • High degree of cooperation among competitor firms to share risk, stabilize market, share innovation. • Disproportionate shares of workers engaged in design, innovation. • Strong trade associations that provide shared infrastructure-management, training, marketing, technical or financial help, i.e., mechanisms for risk sharing and stabilization. • Strong local government role in regulating and promoting core industries.
Hub-and-spoke districts	• Business structure dominated by one or several large, vertically integrated firms surrounded by suppliers. • Core firms embedded non-locally, with substantial links to suppliers and competitors outside of the district. • Scale economies relatively high.

(*Continued*)

Table 2.1. (*Continued*)

Types	Features
	• Low rates of turnover of local business except in third tier.
	• Substantial intra-district trade among dominant firms and suppliers.
	• Key investment decisions made locally, but spread out globally.
	• Long-term contracts and commitments between dominant firms and suppliers.
	• High degrees of cooperation, linkages with external firms both locally and externally.
	• Moderate incidence of exchanges of personnel between customers and suppliers.
	• Low degree of cooperation among large competitor firms to share risk, stabilize market, and share innovation.
	• Labor market internal to the district, less flexible.
	• Disproportionate shares of blue-collar workers.
	• Workers committed to large firms first, then to district, then to small firms.
	• High rates of labor in-migration, but less out-migration.
	• Evolution of unique local cultural identity, bonds.
	• Specialized sources of finance, technical expertise, business services dominated by large firms.
	• Little "patient capital" within district outside of large firms.
	• Absence of trade associations that provide shared infrastructure-management, training, marketing, technical or financial help, i.e., mechanisms for risk sharing and stabilization.
	• Strong local government role in regulating and promoting core industries in local and provincial and national government.
	• High degree of public involvement in providing infrastructure.
	• Long-term prospects for growth dependent upon prospects for the industry and strategies of dominant firms
Satellite industrial platforms	• Business structure dominated by large, externally owned and headquartered firms.
	• Scale economies moderate to high.

(*Continued*)

Table 2.1.   (*Continued*)

Types	Features
	• Low to moderate rates of turnover of platform tenants.
	• Minimal intra-district trade among buyers and suppliers.
	• Key investment decisions made externally.
	• Absence of long-term commitments to suppliers locally.
	• High degrees of cooperation, linkages with external firms, especially with parent company.
	• High incidence of exchanges of personnel between customers and suppliers externally but not locally.
	• Low degree of cooperation among competitor firms to share risk, stabilize market, and share innovation.
	• Labor market external to the district, internal to vertically integrated firm.
	• Workers committed to firm rather than district.
	• High rates of labor in-migration and out-migration at managerial, professional, and technical levels; little at blue-and pink-collar levels.
	• Little evolution of unique local cultural identity, bonds.
	• Main sources of finance, technical expertise, and business services provided externally, through firm or external purchase.
	• No "patient capital" within district.
	• No trade associations that provide shared infrastructure-management, training, marketing, technical, or financial help, i.e., mechanisms for risk sharing and stabilization.
	• Strong local government role in providing infrastructure, tax breaks, and other generic business inducements.
	• Growth jeopardized by intermediate-term portability of plants and activities elsewhere to similarly constructed platforms.
State-anchored industrial districts	• Business structure dominated by one or several large government institutions such as military bases, state or national capitals, large public universities, surrounded by suppliers and customers (including those regulated).
	• Scale economies relatively high in public-sector activities.
	• Low rates of turnover of local business.
	• Substantial intra-district trade among dominant institutions and suppliers, but not among others.

(*Continued*)

Table 2.1. (*Continued*)

Types	Features
	• Key investment decisions made at various levels of government, some internal, some external.
	• Short-term contracts and commitments between dominant institutions and suppliers, customers.
	• High degrees of cooperation, linkages with external firms for externally headquartered supplier organizations.
	• Moderate incidence of exchanges of personnel between customers and suppliers.
	• Low degree of cooperation among local private-sector firms to share risk, stabilize market, and share innovation.
	• Labor market internal if state capital, national if university or military facility or other federal offices for professional/technical and managerial workers.
	• Disproportionate shares of clerical and professional workers.
	• Workers committed to large institutions first, then to district, then to small firms.
	• High rates of labor in-migration, but less out-migration unless government is withdrawing or closing down.
	• Evolution of unique local cultural identity, bonds.
	• No specialized sources of finance, technical expertise, and business services.
	• No "patient capital" within district.
	• Weak trade associations to share information about public-sector client.
	• Weak local government role in regulating and promoting core activities.
	• High degree of public involvement in providing infrastructure.
	• Long-term prospects for growth dependent on prospects for government facilities at core.

Source: Markusen (1996a, 1966b).

are set up in both developing and developed countries through govern-ment initiatives to finance and promote the establishment of local institu-tions such as laboratories, technology diffusion centers, testing centers and R&D facilities (Markusen, 1996a).

Guerrieri and Pietrobelli (2001) classify industrial clusters into casual geographical clustering, Marshallian industrial clusters and enterprise net-work with some form of leadership. Casual geographical clustering arises from occasional inter-firm linkages with limited inter-firm cooperation. Under Marshallian industrial clusters, there are effective local institutions, more frequent inter-firm cooperation, and economies of scale at the district level. In the enterprise network with some form of leadership, some lead-ing firms provide strategic directions for agglomerated SMEs to enter into the range of relevant products, business services and industrial sectors.

Industrial clusters are playing an important part in regional develop-ment of China (Ding, 2006; Bellandi and Lombardi, 2012). The Yangtze River Delta, the Pearl River Delta and Bohai-rim areas have become the most impressive regions in China where industrial clusters have been formed and developed (Li & Fung Research Centre, 2006a; Wei *et al.*, 2009). Currently there are at least three main types of industrial clusters in China, namely, SME industrial clusters, high-tech industrial clusters and export-oriented industrial clusters.

Most SME industrial clusters in China have developed rapidly along the coastal provinces since the mid-1980s. They are mainly labor-intensive with low technology content and low entry barriers. A lot of SMEs are in the form of family businesses. Typical examples include the clothing clus-ter in Ningbo City, the textile cluster in Shaoxing City, the socks cluster in Yiwu City and the hardware cluster in Yongkang City, Zhejiang Province.

High-tech industrial clusters, which first appeared in the early 1980s, are mainly located in the neighborhood of universities and research insti-tutes in the large cities of China. The scientists, scholars and university students have contributed to the formation and development of high-tech industrial clusters. One of the typical examples is Zhongguanchun ICT cluster (ZGC) in Beijing. The rapid growth of ZGC is attributed to its geographical location where a large number of leading research institutes affiliated with Chinese Academy of Sciences agglomerate. Besides, many comprehensive universities including Peking University and Tsinghua

University are located in the surroundings. Many scientists, researchers, local and overseas-returned Chinese talents, who were engaged in high-tech industry, became entrepreneurs and set up their own businesses. The central government and venture capitalists home and abroad have made substantial investments in incubating and cultivating high-tech firms. As a result, ZGC has become one of the largest high-tech R&D research centers and IT products distribution centers in the northern part of China (Zhou *et al.*, 2011).The high-tech development zones, specifically the Economic and Technological Development Zones (ETDZ) in China were primarily designed by the central and local government to promote technology transfer and industrial upgrading (Li, 2009).

Export-oriented industrial clusters have developed with substantial inward foreign direct investment (FDI) to mainland China. For example, Suzhou Industrial Park and Dongguan export-processing zone are typical FDI clustering zones. Globalization has made it possible for multinational corporations (MNCs) to foster global production networks (GPNs). Participation of local enterprises in export-oriented industrial clusters has been conducive for MNCs to develop close ties with local firms. Additionally, FDI industrial clusters are more likely to become innovative clusters (Kim, 2005).

This book will mainly concentrate on the institutional dynamics of SME industrial clusters in East China. The SMEs coexist with large firms and MNCs in the region. Some SMEs will become large firms or MNCs when they grow up. However, the predominance of SMEs will not be changed fundamentally. The inter-firm cooperation not only reduces production costs but also promotes regional knowledge diffusion. There are also supporting institutions such as business associations and universities in the industrial clusters (Wang *et al.*, 2007).

2.3. Competitive Advantage and Industrial Clusters

Industrial clusters are important for stimulating regional development because they can gain both economies of agglomeration and collective efficiency arising from inter-firm linkages. As a result, regional competitiveness can be improved. Industrial clusters have been regarded as one of the effective policy tools and industrial organization means to gain the regional competitiveness in both developed and developing countries.

Porter (1990) developed "diamond" model to analyze national competitive advantage. The framework involves four interactive attributes including factor conditions, demand conditions, related or supporting industries, as well as firm strategy, structure, and rivalry. He argues that domestic rivalry and geographical clustering play an important role in a nation's competitive advantage. Industrial clusters will lead to higher productivity, innovative capability and new venture creation in a region. A clustered firm can be more productive when it has better access to information, technology, R&D research institutions and factors of production. In addition, it can cooperate with other firms in the cluster to combat against the fierce competition outside the region (Porter, 1998). Although Porter's theory has become an important policy tool to promote regional competitiveness, it has aroused wide disputes and received some criticism from the academic circle. Martin and Sunley (2003) argue for a much more cautious use of the concept of industrial cluster particularly within the policy context because it overemphasized the determinants of competitiveness.

The research on the hi-tech industrial clusters in developed countries indicates that talent can only partly contribute to improving the regional competitive advantages. The close inter-firm cooperation in the region has become more important. With a case study of Zhongguanchun high-tech industrial cluster (ZGC) in Beijing, Wang and Wang (1998) argue that the sustainable growth of ZGC is constrained by some negative factors, such as the high hierarchical restraints from the state-owned enterprises and the exposure of local high-tech firms to the fierce world competition after forging close business relationships with MNCs. Indigenous innovation has been highlighted for the sustainable development of hi-tech industrial clusters in developing countries. Fu *et al.* (2009) conducted a comparative study between ZGC in Beijing, China and Silicon Valley in California, USA. The key dimensions of inter-organizational relationship within ZGC such as the labor market, inter-firm linkages, informal social networks, business services and university ties were highlighted. The research indicated that the local high-tech firms were more competitive than the subsidiaries of MNCs in ZGC. The ZGC had some common features as the Silicon Valley such as entrepreneurship, talented workforce, and close collaboration between universities and high-tech firms. However, ZGC and Silicon Valley also demonstrated striking differences in other dimensions such as local governance, information transparency, inter-firm cooperation, the availability of venture capital and the organization of business associations.

With two case studies of ZGC science park and Dongguan PC cluster, He *et al.* (2011) regarded the industrial cluster as a complex adaptive system which goes through self-organization with four important features including landscape design, positive feedback, boundary constraints and novel outcomes. They concluded that both path-dependence and the unpredictability of developmental paths were two important features of cluster development processes in transitional China. Zhou *et al.* (2011) evaluates Harvey's "spatial fix" literature by comparing the spatial patterns and dynamics of three key regions of information and communication industry in China with a large-scale survey conducted in Beijing city, Shanghai–Suzhou area and Shenzhen–Dongguan area in 2006–2007. They found not only obvious regional differences in terms of industrial structures, ownership, export orientation and technological investment, but also a convergence of technological dynamism among foreign and domestic terms in each of the above three regions. There was a negative relationship between multinational corporation-led export industry and technological investments. Although Beijing is the least foreign-oriented region, it outperformed the other two regions considerably in all indicators of technological dynamism. Therefore, they stressed the improtance of indigenous R&D for domestic capital to accelerate the pace of technological innovation in China.

Dijk and Wang (2005) studied a city-wide information and communication technologies (ICTs) cluster in Nanjing City, Jiangsu Province, East China, involving universities, various software parks and a large agglomeration of IT stores. They concluded that the ICT clustering in China was still in an early stage of development. Liu and Song (2006) conducted an empirical study of the home appliance cluster in Qingdao City, Shangdong Province, China. They argued that the development path of this cluster was heavily influenced by the collective innovation of entrepreneurs, including the introduction of new technology and institutional innovation under the firm support by the local government. Cultivating indigenous R&D, participating in the formulation of global standards and joining in global industrial associations are all of vital significance for the internationalization of industrial clusters. Libaers and Meyer (2011) examined the role and differential impact of industrial clustering in the internationalization of small technology-based firms. Serial innovator firms are a set of small, long-lived technology-based firms with a stellar record of inventive success while non-serial innovators are small technology-based firms with much weaker inventive capabilities. By synthesizing the resource-based view and density dependence theory, they conclude that both serial and non-serial innovator firms benefit from rising levels of industrial clustering in their efforts to internationalize. But non-serial innovators experience decreasing returns with increasing levels of clustring. The overall serial innovator firms benefit more from industrial clustering in terms of internationalization than non-serial innovator firms because all small technology-based firms are not the same and serial innovators are more effective at leveraging cluster-based resources than non-serial innovators, even when they operate in the same industry.

Wei *et al.* (2009) analyzed the transformation of Suzhou City, Jiangsu Province, known previously for its South Jiangsu model of development, into a globalizing foreign direct investment (FDI) and high-technology center. They argued that the key to the transformation has been the efforts of states in utilizing global capital, mainly through the development of the Suzhou Industrial Park (SIP). However, the nature of SIP is largely that of a satellite district, and its future is likely a satellite neo-Marshallian district. A third pathway of development is promoted by globalizing regional development while domesticating globalization, and by moving beyond the divide of localization and globalization.

Taiwan has witnessed the successful development of hi-tech industrial clusters and accumulated rich experiences of incubating hi-tech firms. Hsu (2010) examined the late-industrialization paradigm by exploring high-technology development in Taiwan. The latercomer advantage was constructed based on learning and strong state intervention. In spite of being praised as a model of the developmental statist paradigm as in South Korea, the development of high-technology industry in Taiwan demonstrated a different path of late-industrialization. The industrial system in Taiwan was characterized by vertical disintegration, learning networks and redundant institutional embeddedness. The high-technology industries in Taiwan revealed an advantage of flexible specialization and collaborative learning in the deepening globalization. In particular, the connections between the social and professional communities in Taiwan and Silicon

Valley provided a bridge for technological cooperation and enhanced the learning capabilities of latecomer firms. In other words, the central agent of the rapid growth of high-technology industry in Taiwan was the technical community instead of the large MNCs in South Korea. Hsu (2004) explored the process of institutional change in the globalization of late-industrial district in Taiwan. The high-tech industrial system in Taiwan is noted for its decentralization and geographical agglomeration. It demonstrates varieties of features of industrial districts including spin-offs, collaborations, networking, and institutional presences. At the initial stage, the government in Taiwan led in technology transfer, encouraged new venture creation and encouraged the private sector to bring the industry into being. However, as the industry became global, new complementary institutions, including dense social and professional connections and associations, replaced the monotonic role of the local state to make learning through networks effective in the decentralized industrial system.

Some research has focused on the development and upgrading of industrial clusters in China along the GVC. Zhang (2006) explored how local industrial clusters climb up the GVC and participate in global competition. Three types of driving mechanism in global industrial transfer and division of labor were highlighted including producer-driven, buyer-driven and a hybrid form. The formation and upgrading paths of industrial clusters differed under the above three driving mechanisms. The upgrading of local industrial clusters was also constrained by three models of chain governance including a market system, a hierarchical system and a quasi-hierarchical system. After this discussion, he created one spatial hierarchical system of local industrial clusters in the GVC, illustrated by the example of Shanghai's diffusion over Zhejiang province and Jiangsu province. According to his ideas, most of the industries in China were still at the lower end of value chain. Since the industrial upgrading was a dynamic process, the innovation corresponding to the present development stage in China would promote the upgrading of local industrial clusters. The case study of Zhejiang Pinghu optical and electrical cluster indicated that the small firms around one leading firm in the industrial cluster could diffuse technological innovation into the whole industrial organization and lead to the eventual upgrading of entire industrial cluster. Mei *et al.* (2006) studied the role of knowledge flow in the upgrading of industrial clusters along the GVC. Since most of industrial clusters in China were labor-intensive, their sustainable development is constrained by excessive competition and brand absence. Therefore, effective knowledge management could enhance the competitiveness of industrial clusters and promote the regional economic development. They argue that integrating different types of technology and market channels can lead to the upgrading of industrial clusters along the GVC.

The definition of organizational proximity goes beyond simple geographical proximity. They attach much importance to the integration of diverse production activities along the GVC. The integration can help reduce transactions costs, create local capabilities and generate a shared vision of business growth and potential from various possible technological trajectories. Global economic integration indicates that the access to international markets is not achieved merely by designing, making and marketing new products alone for many industries. Instead, it involves gaining entry into international design, production and marketing networks that are composed of many different firms. Wang (2008) argues that the development of supporting industries plays an important role in creating linkages between multinational companies and firms in the industrial clusters in China, thereby stimulating the competitiveness of downstream industries there. The research shows that the adjustments of international strategies by multinational companies have great impacts on their organizational structures.

The Pearl River Delta Model was driven by the inflows of manufacturing investment from Hong Kong and Taiwan in the 1980s and 1990s. Its development path has been reshaped by the trans-local dynamics since 2000 including institutional interactions between home and host regions within the GPNs (Yang, 2007). Yang and Liao (2010) compared the emergence and patterns of industrial clustering in the IT sector of Dongguan City, Guangdong Province, which has enjoyed substantial investment from Taiwan. They argued that the investment from Taiwan has demonstrated distinctive development trajectories in terms of production systems, technological upgrading and the embeddedness to the local economy. The case study of Taiwan IT firms in Dongguan City also suggests that the cultural affinity and kin relations continue to affect the embeddedness of overseas Chinese investment in the mainland, even though its role has been changing in the context of globalization and local economic restructuring. Kim and Zhang (2008) investigated the clustering of Chinese electronics manufacturers with foreign producers in Qingdao City, North China and examine how the supplier–buyer linkages between foreign invested enterprises and local firms have led to the formation of a successful electronics industry cluster in the industrial development zones. They argued that the secret of Chinese electronic producers' success depends on their ability to drive, instead of being subordinate to, the industrial network.

Networks are the means by which firms in one area are developed into industrial clusters. The principal task of networks is to gather and spread information. Networks have been identified as crucial elements within the local production system. Zhu and Gai (2001) discovered that traditional industrial clusters, with local industrial networks established on the basis of social networks in certain areas, possess strong learning capacities and exhibit similar features to those in developed countries. Cai and Wu (2008) have re-examined the logic of the competitive advantage of industrial clusters coupled with the evolution of the business environment, analyzing the relationships between the network structure, the dynamic network capabilities and competitive advantage of industrial clusters from the inter-firm network perspective and provide a structuralist cluster theory based on the micro-data. The functioning mechanism of network structure and associated dynamic network capabilities in improving the competitive advantages of industrial clusters were tested with the empirical data from nine textile clusters in Zhejiang Province using social networks analysis, providing a coherent understanding of the structural functions of the inter-firm network as well as the formation and evolution of industrial clusters. Wang (2009) studied the relationship between the inter-regional expansion of firms and upgrading of industrial clusters using the same perspective. Network resources provide advantages for industrial clusters, but the evolution of network resources can also bring about a "lock-in" effect and obstruct the development of regional economy. Using the analytical framework of social networks, they argue that the inter-regional expansion of clustered firms will change and extend the network structure of industrial cluster. The transformation of network structure will promote the improvement of network resources for clustered firms, enhance the position of industrial clusters in the GPN and eventually realize the upgrading of industrial clusters.

Li (2006) analyzed the relationships between the firm, the innovations of network organization and the governance of industrial clusters. The organizational structure of industrial clusters depends upon the interactive relationship among clustered firms. Creating boundaryless organizations makes the industrial cluster more flexible and adaptable to changes in the external environment, leading to organizational innovation and allowing the cluster to further adapt to changes in the knowledge economy. Wang (2006) studied the technological innovation of clustered firms, network embeddedness and cluster upgrading in the Chinese manufacturing industry. He argued that the improvement in the technological innovation capability of domestic clustered firms provides the micro-foundation and basic propelling power for upgrading the Chinese manufacturing clusters. Different forms of network embeddedness among the manufacturing clusters provide the foundation stones for supporting different learning modes and gaining different types of knowledge. The research analyzed the technological innovation capacities of domestic clustered firms during the cluster upgrading process, clarified the different types of knowledge and learning modes supporting the different technological innovation levels and developed different network embeddedness patterns. Zhang *et al.* (2011) adopted a cognitive community-based analytic framework to study the intra-cluster knowledge diffusion within Datang socks cluster in Zhejiang Province, East China. They argued that the initial pattern of knowledge distribution influences the process of knowledge diffusion in a cluster significantly. A cluster with a higher knowledge level but lower knowledge heterogeneity has higher efficiency of knowledge diffusion.

Zeng and Si (2008) studied the financial services cluster in the Lujiazui area of Shanghai City, which consists of a large number of financial firms and supporting intermediary firms. There are both competition and cooperation within this highly agglomerating industrial grouping. The research suggests that the inter-firm network there exhibits more openness than traditional industrial clusters. They conclude that this financial cluster is still in its initial stage and that its competitiveness can be enhanced with the further development of the financial industry and better integration of new entrants with local clustered firms.

2.4. Institutional Change and the Development of Industrial Clusters

The development of industrial clusters in China is closely related to location, competition, technology and institutions (Fig. 2.1). This book focuses

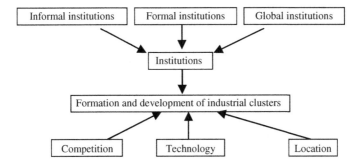

Fig. 2.1.   Theoretical framework of the research.
Source: Compiled by the author.

principally on the institutional dimension of SME cluster development in East China. The institutions are decomposed into informal, formal and global institutions. As the neo-classical economics mainly concentrate on the economic issues within a given institutional environment, it cannot interpret transitional economies undergoing fundamental and diverse institutional change thoroughly. The research fills in the gap by studying how institutional change affects the formation and development of textile and clothing clusters in Zhejiang Province, East China and contribute to a better understanding of institutional change and regional development in transitional China.

Institutional theories deal with institutions, uncertainties and processes in divergent ways. The well-known distinction of institutional theories lies in the old institutionalism and New Institutional Economics (NIE). The old institutionalism was predominant in the first half of the 20th century and represented by Veblen (1898), Commons (1934) and Mitchell (1937). The old institutionalists preferred inductive theorizing and demonstrated the similarities to the German Historical Schools (Mortel, 2002). The NIE can be divided into two broad schools. The first school concentrates on the choice of governance structures for private actors under an institutional environment, which is assumed to be given. It is concerned with investigating the conditions within which exchange will be secured at least cost through the market and the conditions within which exchange will be secured within organizations. The analytic tradition was initiated by Coase (1937) and reinvigorated by Williamson (1985). The simple dichotomy between firms and the market has been transformed into a continuum through fine-grained governance structures such as long-term contracts. The second school does not take the institutional environment as given, but investigates the effects that various institutional environments have on economic performance and development as well as explaining the change of the institutional environment over time. The representatives of the second school include Douglas North, Richard Posner, Andrew Schotter and Richard Nelson (Powell and Dimaggio, 1991). The NIE has advanced a basic concept of transaction costs as the fundamental cause of institutional change, which is further developed in the property rights school (Coase, 1960; Williamson, 1985).

Ruttan and Hayami (1984) argue that the demand for institutional change results from technological change, factor endowments and production requirements while the supply of institutional change is determined by the cost of gaining a consensus within the whole society, which, in turn, depends on the power structure of vested interest groups. In the theory of self-reinforcing mechanisms, Arthur (1988) compares four types of mechanism inducing institutional change including large set-up or fixed costs, which give the advantage of falling unit costs as output increases; learning effects, which improve products or reduce their costs as their prevalence increases; coordination effects, which confer advantages to cooperate with other economic agents taking similar actions; and adaptive expectations, where the anticipation of market changes can be reinforced by the beliefs of agents. The consequence of these self-reinforcing mechanisms is characterized by four properties including multiple equilibrium, in which a number of solutions are possible and the outcome is indeterminate; possible inefficiencies, in which a technology that is inherently better than another loses out because of bad luck in gaining adherence; lock-in, in which a solution is difficult to exit from once reached; path dependence, in which the consequence of small events and chanced circumstances can determine the solutions that lead one to a particular path once they prevail.

According to North (1990), institutions are rules of the game. There are millions of games that govern our social, political and economic life and interact in complex ways to affect economic performance. The aim of members of organizations is to improve their chances in the game. For this purpose, they may wish to change the rules to their own advantage. But, even if they succeed, institutional change is likely to be marginal since there will be few groups with sufficient bargaining power against others to bend institutions in their favor. While formal institutions normally change marginally, they can still be replaced overnight. However, informal institutions always tend to change only marginally since norms and values tend to be remarkably stable. When decisions do not depend on the past or on learning, the concept of development paths is not useful. But when information is incomplete or there is uncertainty, development paths are important. When these paths vary, decisions can be different even if circumstances are otherwise similar. Therefore, the concept of path dependency is not deterministic.

Some Chinese scholars have developed the theory of institutional change in the context of economic development in China. For example, Lin (1989) used the concepts of induced institutional change and imposed institutional change. Because of limited human rationality and free-rider problem, the supply of institutions caused by induced institutional change fails to reach the social optimal level and the government has to take advantage of imposed institutional change to remedy this. Yang (1993) distinguished between supply-dominant and demand-induced institutional change. Supply-dominant institutional change is enforced by the government on a top-down basis. Additionally, he argued for a theory of institutional change involving three stages including supply dominant, intermediate diffusion and demand induced. He argued that China is currently in the stage of intermediate diffusion and would not reach the demand-induced stage until enterprises had the capacity to bear the costs of institutional innovation. Zhou (2000) made use of Hayek's theory of dualism and drew the conclusion that institutional evolution in China was, in fact, an evolutionary process involving conflicts and coordination between internal and external rules and that those internal rules play a critical role in the formation of social order. Qian (2000) explored the institutional foundation of China's market transition from 1978 to 1998. He argued that the main lesson learned from the Chinese experience is that considerable growth is possible with sensible but not perfect institutions, and that some unconventional transitional institutions can be more effective than the best practice institutions for a period of time because of the second-best principle. Specific lessons include incentives, hard budget constraints, and competition should apply not only to firms but also to governments; reforms can be implemented without creating many or big losers; and successful reforms require appropriate, but not necessarily optimal sequencing.

The economic transition in China has been driven by the interaction among the state, foreign capital and localities. The formation and development of industrial clusters have taken place under the triple transition of decentralization, marketization and globalization (Wei, 2000). Currently, much research has been done on how to design, implement and assess cluster policies in China, ignoring the fact that the formation and development of industrial clusters have resulted from the interaction between informal, formal and global institutional forces. It remains unclear how clustered firms will respond and how they will perform in a society where the institutional environment continues to evolve. The business system in China is the outcome of interaction between the exogenous international institutions such as the regulations of the WTO, the exogenous macro-level institutions such as the fiscal stimulus, and the endogenous micro-level institutions such as organizational change (Krug and Hendrischke, 2008). The evolution of micro-level institutions in the business sector induces demand for more effective macro-level institutions while international institutional change such as the deepening globalization and global financial turmoil affects both the macro-level and micro-level institutions in China. The book specifically looks into the interaction among informal, formal and global institutions in the course of the development and upgrading of textile and clothing clusters in rural China.

2.5. Conclusion

The academic circle in China did not embark on research into industrial clusters until the early 1990s. The previous literature mainly focuses on the economic performance of industrial clusters and their impacts on the regional development in China. The research on industrial clusters in China has been extended in terms of innovation, internationalization, competitive advantage and global value chain and so on. The research adopts a multi-dimensional institution approach to examine how the interaction between informal, formal and international institutional change affects the formation and development of textile and clothing industrial clusters in rural China.

3

GLOBAL INSTITUTIONAL CHANGE AND THE DEVELOPMENT OF TEXTILE AND CLOTHING CLUSTERS IN CHINA

3.1. Introduction

China is one of the major players in the textile and clothing industry in the world currently, accounting for 23.5% in world exports of textiles and 33.4% in world exports of garments in 2007 (see Tables 3.1 and 3.2). The combined textile imports of the United States, the EU and Canada from China rose by 41% in 2005. More than three quarters of Japan's textile and clothing imports originated from China in 2006. Although the introduction of quotas by the United States and the EU in the course of 2005 had a restrictive effect on textiles imports from China, China's overall exports of textiles and clothing to the world increased by 25% in 2006, which was higher than 21% in 2005 (WTO, 2007).

Since the 1980s, the country has attracted textile and clothing manufacturers all over the world to set up production bases because of the abundant supply of cheap and skilled labor. As explained above, the textile and clothing clusters are primarily located in the coastal regions, particularly in the Yangtze River Delta, the Pearl River Delta and Bohairim region. Hundreds of textile and clothing manufacturers have clustered together in each of these localities. Firms of supporting industries are also located in the same region. The commodity trading markets serve as important trading platforms for textile and clothing firms in the above

Table 3.1.   Leading exporters of textiles in 2010 (billion dollars and percentage).

Exporters	Value 2010	Share in world exports/imports 1980	1990	2000	2010
China[a]	77	4.6	6.9	10.4	30.7
European Union (27)	67	—	—	36.6	26.8
Extra-EU(27) exports	21	—	—	10.1	8.3
India	13	2.4	2.1	3.6	5.1
The United State	12	6.8	4.8	7.1	4.9
Hong Kong, China	11	—	—	—	—
Domestic exports	0	1.7	2.1	0.8	0.1
Re-exports	11	—	—	—	—
Korea, Republic of	11	4.0	5.8	8.2	4.4
Taipei, Chinese	10	3.2	5.9	7.7	3.9
Turkey	9	0.6	1.4	2.4	3.6
Pakistan	8	1.6	2.6	2.9	3.1
Japan	7	9.3	5.6	4.5	2.8
Indonesia	4	0.1	1.2	2.3	1.7
Thailand	4	0.6	0.9	1.3	1.5
Vietnam[b]	3	—	—	0.2	1.1
Mexico[a]	2	0.2	0.7	1.7	0.8
Canada	2	0.6	0.7	1.4	0.8
Above 15	**228**	—	—	**91.0**	**91.1**

Notes: (a) Includes significant shipments through processing zones; (b) Includes Secretariat estimates.
Source: WTO (2011).

regions. In a globalizing world where private firms in China have to compete internationally, the textile and clothing clusters are playing an important role in supporting firms' competitiveness by increasing productivity and encouraging innovation. This chapter reviews the historic development of the textile and clothing industry and cluster development in China, and then elaborates on the impact of international institutional change on them.

Table 3.2.   Leading exporters of clothing in 2010 (billion dollars and percentage).

Exporters	Value 2010	Share in world exports/imports 1980	1990	2000	2010
China[a]	130	4.0	8.9	18.3	36.9
European Union (27)	99	—	—	28.5	28.1
Extra-EU (27) exports	22	—	—	6.6	6.3
Hong Kong, China	24	—	14.2	—	—
Domestic exports	0	11.5	8.6	5.0	0.1
Re-exports	24	0	5.7	—	—
Bangladesh[b]	16	0.	3.1	2.6	4.5
Turkey	13	0.3	0.6	3.3	3.6
India	11	1.7	2.3	3.0	3.2
Vietnam[b]	11	—	…	0.9	3.1
Indonesia	7	0.2	1.5	2.4	1.9
United States	5	3.1	0.5	4.4	1.3
Mexico[a]	4	0.0	2.4	4.4	1.2
Thailand	4	0.7	2.6	1.9	1.2
Pakistan	4	0.3	0.9	1.1	1.1
Malaysia[a]	4	0.4	0.7	1.1	1.1
Sri Lanka[b]	3	0.3	1.0	1.4	1.0
Tunisia[b]	3	0.8	0.6	1.4	0.9
Above 15	**314**	—	—	79.5	89.4

Notes: (a) Includes significant shipments through processing zones; (b) Includes Secretariat estimates.
Source: WTO (2011).

3.2. The Development of the Textile and Clothing Industry in China

The textile and clothing industry, one of the backbone industries in China, has played an important part in national industrialization and export growth after China's adoption of open-door policy in 1978. The production of textiles and clothing is relatively concentrated in the eastern part of China, particularly Zhejiang, Jiangsu, Shandong, Guangdong and Fujian provinces as well as Shanghai. The eastern part of China accounted for 73% of total employment, 88% of total exports and more than 90% of FDI in the textiles and clothing sector in China in 2007 (CNTAC, 2007a). Shangdong and Jiangsu provinces are relatively rich in cotton production compared with other coastal provinces. The cotton output of Zhejiang province amounted to only 62,000 tons in 1996, 40,000 tons in 2000, 21,000 tons in 2004 and 24,000 tons in 2007. Guangdong and Fujian provinces do not produce any cotton at all (see Table 3.3). However, the textile and garments output in the three provinces has been in the front rank of China. For example, the profits of large-scale textile enterprises and the output of main textile products in Zhejiang province were ranked the first in 2001 (see Tables 3.4 and 3.5). The statistics has shown that the resources are not the critical factor leading to the success of textile and clothing clusters in Zhejiang, Fujian and Guangdong provinces. The critical determinants must lie in location and other institutional factors including the norms, culture, entrepreneurship and behavior of local government. These typical institutional factors will be explored further in the following chapters.

In the 1980s, the textile and clothing producers from Japan, Hong Kong, Taiwan and South Korea, started to invest heavily in Guangdong province in an attempt to meet the demands of both their domestic markets as well as overseas markets in Western Europe and North America and offset the rising wage costs in their home countries. Subsequently, foreign capital flowed steadily to the Yangtze River Delta, including Shanghai, Zhejiang province and Jiangsu province (Li & Fung Research Centre, 2006b).

In the mid-1990s, the state-owned textile industry became the worst performing industrial sector in China. Losses in the industry reached USD1.3 billion in 1996. Many factors led to the faltering of the industry. First, there was overstocking of textile products within SOEs due to the overcapacity in the 1980s and early 1990s while local governments made blind investments in the repetitive construction of textile plants all over the country. By the mid-1990s, consumers' behavior in the domestic market started to change as living standards continued to improve. They attached more importance to the quality of textiles and style of clothes

Table 3.3.   The provincial output of cotton in China from 1996–2007 (Unit: 10,000 tons).

	1996	2000	2004	2007
Beijing	0.3	0.2	0.3	0.2
Tianjin	1.1	0.6	9.5	10.9
Hebei	37.0	22.3	52.2	62.8
Shanxi	9.1	4.4	9.2	11.8
Inner Mongolia	0.0	0.2	0.5	0.2
Liaoning	2.4	0.5	0.3	0.2
Jilin	0.0	0.0	0.1	0.3
Heilongjiang	0.0	0.0	0.0	0.0
Shanghai	0.4	0.2	0.1	0.2
Jiangsu	56.2	24.6	29.1	38.1
Zhejiang	6.2	4.0	2.1	2.4
Anhui	30.1	19.5	24.1	40.8
Fujian	0.0	0.0	0.0	0.0
Jiangxi	11.9	6.3	7.6	9.5
Shandong	47.1	33.9	87.7	102.3
Henan	77.0	70.7	37.7	83.0
Hubei	58.6	28.2	32.5	44.9
Hunan	22.4	17.7	16.3	24.8
Guangdong	0.0	0.0	0.0	0.0
Guangxi	0.1	0.1	0.1	0.1
Hainan	0.0	0.0	0.0	0.0
Chongqing		0.1	0.0	0.0
Sichuan	11.2	7.6	2.5	1.6
Guizhou	0.1	0.1	0.1	0.1
Yunnan	0.1	0.1	0.0	0.0
Tibet	0.0	0.0	0.0	0.0
Shanxi	4.0	2.0	5.3	8.7
Gansu	2.3	4.3	8.7	12.8
Qinghai	0.0	0.0	0.0	0.0
Ningxia	0.0	0.0	0.0	0.0
Xinjiang	99.4	135.4	160.0	218.9

Sources: National Bureau of Statistics of China (1996, 2000, 2004, 2006).

Table 3.4.   The ratio and ranking of main economic indicators of large-scale textile enterprises of Zhejiang province in China.

Indicators	2001 Ratio in China (percent)	Ranking	1996 Ratio in China (percent)	Ranking
Number of units	19.3	2	12.1	2
Added-value of industry	15.3	2	11.7	3
Total assets	14.5	2	10.9	3
Sales revenue	20.0	2	12.3	2
Total profits	36.1	1	The whole China suffered from a loss of RMB7.13 billion while Zhejiang province made a profit of RMB382 million.	2
Employees	11.8	3	9.3	3

Source: Zhang (2003).

rather than having merely enough to wear. More than 1,000 out of an estimated 3,277 state-owned textile enterprises were idle or partially idle in the first quarter of 1996. Second, the fast increase of spinning capacity resulted in fierce fight for raw materials among the textile firms throughout the country. The price of cotton increased by 38% in 1993 and rose well above the average international price. The price of synthetic fiber was also on the rise, weakening the cost advantages of state-owned textile and clothing firms. Third, many other developing countries competed against China in the low- and medium-grade textile markets. Though exports of textile and clothing products were increasing, the net revenue of foreign exchange dropped. Moreover, the management and operation of state-owned textile enterprises were inefficient. Under the centrally planned economy, workers could enjoy permanent occupational status and a package of social welfare including housing, health and pensions from their work units. Gradually, state-owned textile enterprises found it difficult to

Table 3.5.   The market share and ranking of Zhejiang textile industry in China in 2001.

Textile products	Output in Zhejiang province	The ratio of Zhejiang province in China (percent)	Ranking
Pure synthetic fabrics (100 million meters)	16.32	37.28	1
Printing and dyeing fabrics (100 million meters)	81.84	45.90	1
Raw silk (10,000 tons)	4.43	49.11	1
Silk weaving products (100 million meters)	29.60	63.23	1
Printing and dyeing silk weaving products (100 million meters)	10.80	55.70	1
Cotton weaving products (10,000 tons)	14.72	21.64	1
Non-weaving fabrics (10,000 tons)	2.02	32.48	1
Socks (100 million pairs)	82.00	65.00	1

Source: China Textile Industrial Association (2002).

compete against joint ventures and private enterprises. The state-owned textile enterprises usually had three times as many employees as the foreign-funded enterprises (FFE), but the productivity per worker was less than half that of their rivals. There was also a widening productivity gap between state-owned and foreign-funded clothing firms (Wei *et al.*, 2002). In 1999, the state-owned textile sector alone was making a loss of RMB 2.15 billion (see Table 3.6).

When the Ninth Five-Year Plan started in 1996, both central and local governments began to promote the necessary structural adjustment by creating a new system for the textile and clothing industry (Table 3.7). The SOEs were stabilized to RMB3 million when they eliminated 10,000 spindles. The reserve funds of state-owned banks were the main source of this financial subsidy. Loans with favorable interest rates were offered by local fiscal bureau, and they could be repaid in five to seven years. In addition, the central government imposed strict controls on the production of

Table 3.6. Comparison of state-owned and foreign-funded textiles and clothing enterprises in 1999.

	Enterprises	Employees/ enterprise	Value added (RMB billion)	Sales (RMB billion)	Profits (RMB billion)	Productivity per employee (RMB)
Textiles/SOE	3,011	903	41.70	148.24	−2.15	15,325
Textiles/FFE	2,032	299	23.41	88.30	1.29	38.496
Garments/SOE	792	303	4.04	13.52	0.17	16,833
Garments/FFE	2,864	332	24.52	90.91	2.64	25,800

Notes: The annual sales of enterprises in the table exceeded RMB5 million. The productivity is measured as value added per employee.
Source: National Bureau of Statistics of China (2000).

Table 3.7. Objectives and fulfillment of reforming the state-owned textile enterprises in China during 1996–2000.

Targets	Fulfillment by the end of 2000
To eliminate 10 million outdated cotton spindles.	9.4 million cotton spindles and 280,000 wool spindles were eliminated.
To lay off 1.2 million textile workers.	1.4 million people were laid off.
To turn deficits into profits.	The profits reached RMB6.7 billion.

Source: Wei *et al.* (2002).

new cotton spindles. The manufacture, sales and imports of looms were strictly administered and managed by the issuance of production certificates, purchase certificates and import certificates (Wei *et al.*, 2002).

The international competitiveness of the textile industry in China was further weakened during the Asian financial crisis as a result of fierce competition from countries in Southeastern Asia. In order to encourage textile exports, the Ministry of Commerce raised the rate of export rebates for textiles exports uniformly from 9% to 11% from 1 January 1998. The export of textile machinery and equipment could enjoy full tax rebates and preferential credit guarantee treatment. Meanwhile, non-state-owned textile enterprises started to expand their business rapidly. The share of the state-owned sector declined considerably from 67% in 1985 to 30% in 2000.

Meanwhile, the share of joint-ventures, collective and private firms reached 29%, 26% and 15% respectively in 2000. These policies achieved the expected results. By the end of 2000, about 9.4 million cotton spindles and 280,000 wool spindles had been eliminated; 1.4 million textile workers had been laid off and the profits of state-owned textile enterprises had reached RMB6.7 billion (see Table 3.7). Although the number of state-owned textile enterprises had been declining in relative terms, it still played an important role in the development of the textile industry (Wei *et al.*, 2002).

After China joined the World Trade Organization at the end of 2001, the exports of textile and clothing products hit USD88.767 billion in 2004 and USD107.661 billion in 2005 (see Table 3.8). The industry created a trade surplus of USD657.6 billion and USD842.16 billion respectively. As a result, the textile and clothing industry has become one of the most important contributors to the overall trade surplus in China. The total export value of Zhejiang, Jiangsu, Shanghai, Guangdong, Fujian and Shangdong Province amounted to USD19.4 billion in 2004, accounting for 81.5% of total textile and clothing exports in China, with the textile production representing 53% and the clothing 47% (CNTAC, 2005). The clothing sector is more export-oriented than the textile sector. The clothing sector makes slightly higher profit margins than the textile sector because clothing involves more added value with regard to design and production differentiation components than the textile products which are mostly semi-finished items. The rapid expansion of China's exports of textiles and clothing to the rest of world has been closely linked to the phenomenon of industrial clustering of textiles and clothing firms at the Yangtze River Delta and the Pearl River Delta, which has important economic and social implications for the Chinese economy. Most of the textile and clothing clusters have witnessed rapid development and the clustered firms are trying to expand their businesses and create their own original brands in addition to undertaking OEM. The textile and clothing clusters are moving towards higher positions on the value chains and improving their competitiveness.

However, the textiles and clothing industry in China continues to face some challenges. Currently, China is mainly exporting low- and middle-end textile and clothing products with low profit margins. The technological innovation is very limited in the industry. In addition, there are still

Table 3.8.   Value of imports and exports of textile materials and products in China in 2009–2010 (Customs Statistics, USD100 million).

Categories of Commodities	2009		2010	
	Exports	Imports	Exports	Imports
Textile materials and products	1614.09	217.80	1995.33	295.80
Natural Silk	12.90	1.09	16.42	1.24
Wool; Wool yarn and Woolen woven fabrics	16.26	22.15	23.62	28.28
Cotton	96.07	61.80	130.67	106.21
Other textile fiber; Yarn and related woven fabrics	5.93	3.96	8.70	5.60
Synthetic fiber; Continuous filament	74.95	32.1	100.85	37.84
Synthetic fiber; Staple fiber	60.61	25.09	79.57	30.19
Wadding; Felt and Adhesive-bond fabrics; Special yarn; Thread; rope; Cable and Related products	19.62	8.99	26.83	11.27
Carpets and Related products	14.90	1.02	19.55	1.30
Special woven fabrics; Lace; Embroidery	35.26	6.20	38.05	6.94
Coated textiles; Textile products for industrial use	39.67	15.08	36.26	18.47
Knitwear and Crocheted fabrics	64.23	21.37	86.67	23.46
Knitted or Crocheted garments & Clothing accessories	538.14	6.33	667.10	8.18
Garments not knitted or crocheted	467.30	10.20	543.61	14.20
Other textile products; Second-hand garments	168.25	2.42	197.44	2.62

Sources: National Bureau of Statistics of China (2011).

shortages of key production inputs such as electricity and cotton. Moreover, China has to nurture its own famous brands in the international market.

In April 2006, the NDRC, MOFCOM and eight other government departments issued a circular setting out targets to accelerate the restructuring of the textile industry so as to raise labor productivity by 60% between

2006 and 2010, and reduce energy and water intensity by 20%. In June 2006, the CNTAC and the NDRC issued the Development Guidelines for the Textile Industry in the 11th Five-Year Period (2006–2010), which proposed upgrading the technology and increasing the production of high-quality products, developing energy-saving techniques, and promoting the development of the industry in central and western China. In the same year, the central government made an investment of RMB1.36 billion to improve productivity in the textile and clothing industry and RMB560 million to promote innovation and support enterprises to go abroad and expand in other developing and the least developed countries (WTO, 2008).

3.3. The Evolution of Global Textile and Clothing Trade Regime

Under the auspices of the GATT in 1962, the developed countries and developing nations reached a Long-Term Arrangement regarding International Trade in Cotton, Textiles and Substitutes. It was replaced by the Multifibre Arrangement (MFA) in 1974. The MFA (1974–1994) provided for the application of selective quantitative restrictions when surges in imports of particular products caused, or threatened to cause, serious damage to the industry of the importing country. It was an explicit attempt to protect developed country producers by restricting exports of textiles and clothing from developing to developed countries. Theoretically, it sought to provide temporary protection to textile and clothing firms in developed countries to undertake the necessary changes so as to compete against lower cost producers from developing countries in due course. In practice, the MFA not only provided an effective framework for extending the protected position of garment manufacturers in developed countries, but also gave some LDCs preferential quota access to the leading markets around the world. However, the MFA was a major departure from the basic GATT rules, particularly the principle of non-discrimination (WTO, 2008).

On 1 January 1995, the MFA was replaced by the WTO Agreement on Textiles and Clothing (ATC), which set out a transitional process for the ultimate removal of quotas outside GATT rules at the end of 2004. The transitional program has been done in four stages over a period of

10 years under the agreement, allowing those countries affected by the MFA to take steps to make adjustments to a new "free-trade" environment. It was designed to terminate the series of trade-distorting regimes that had governed textile and clothing trade over some four decades. On 1 January 2005, all special quotas on textile and clothing were finally eliminated for member countries of the WTO (WTO, 2008). However, the global textiles and clothing trade has not been undertaken in a quota free environment.

3.4. The Impacts of Global Institutional Change on the Textile and Clothing Clusters in China

International institutional change imposes great impacts on the sustainable growth and upgrading of textile and clothing clusters in China. The removal of quantitative restrictions does not imply unconstrained trade in textiles and clothing. Indeed, the level of tariffs on textiles and clothing remains high even after the reductions were implemented as a result of Uruguay Round Commitments.

The United States negotiated a market access agreement with China, which became part of China's Protocol of Accession to the WTO in December 2001. The agreement includes a textile-specific safeguard provision allowing the imposition of quotas on imports of textile and clothing from China that causes or threatens to cause market disruption. This agreement did not expire until the end of 2008. On 1 January 2002, the United States abolished quantitative import restrictions on 12 clothing categories for the third stage of ATC-integration including baby wear, cotton dressing gowns and bathrobes, gloves made of man-made fibers, brassieres, dressing gowns and bathrobes of man-made fibers, silk gloves, silk mens' coats, silk womens' coats, silk dresses, silk woven skirts and silk trousers. These 12 categories accounted for about 8% of the United States imports of MFA-categories in terms of value, about 4% in terms of volume in 2001. The strong growth of imports in the 12 liberalized categories from China to the United States led to a more than five-fold rise in market share for mainland China to reach almost 60% on average for these categories in terms of both value and volume between 2001 and mid-2004. In December 2003, the United States implemented import quotas on China's export on five categaries, three of which had been liberalized in 2002, including knit fabric, cotton and man-made fiber brassieres, cotton and man-made fiber dressing gowns (Mayer, 2005).

The Memorandum of Understanding between the Governments of the United States of America and the People's Republic of China Concering Trade in Textile and Apparel Products was reached on 1 January 2006 and expired on 31 December 2008.

It covers 34 categories of textiles and apparel imports from China with 21 annual absolute quota limits (OTEXA, 2013).

Quantitative restrictions for 11 categories were affected by the third stage of ATC-integration in the European Union (EU) on 1 January 2002 including gloves, underwear, parkas, nightwear, women or girls' skirts, pile fabrics, synthetic filament fabrics, fabrics of continuous artificial fibers, fabrics of continuous staple fibers, babywear and tracksuits (WTO, 2001). The value of imports from mainland China rose, sometimes very substantially, for all these categories in the EU in 2003 and 2004. However, the growth rates of imports originating in greater China area was about half that for mainland China alone in 2002 and 2003. Hence, part of the increase in the value of EU-imports from China reflected substitution of imports from mainland China that had been previously channeled through the Hong Kong China Special Administrative Region, Macao China Special Administrative Region, or Taiwan. The countries with preferential access to the EU-market through regional trading agreements such as Turkey, the Eastern European and the North African countries succeeded in maintaining their market shares. The regulations through which the EU grants tariff preferences to these countries helped shield them from competitive pressure from China. The EU also used unilaterally determined measures designed to limit a rise in China's market share in textile and clothing trade. The re-imposition of quotas on textile and clothing imports from China by the United States and EU stopped the rise of China's shares in the United States and European countries. Besides, the contradiction between global free trade and regional trade agreements became much fiercer (Mayer, 2005).

As a results, China implemented a series of measures to control textile exports, including imposing export tariffs on 148 categories of textiles and apparel products and strengthening self regulation among textile firms and exporters in 2005. Ministry of Finance in China rasied the export tariffs on certain categories of textiles from 1 June 2005 (Wei, 2005).

More and more industrial clusters in China target international markets as the main destination for their products, but most clustered firms are still at the bottom of the international division of labor. Although a large number of labor-intensive clustered firms have strong international competitiveness, they rely principally on low-price competition. The constant low-price competition not only affects the bargaining power associated with export earnings, but also results in trade frictions. The further implementation of an export-oriented strategy by China has also been constrained by other developing countries that can enjoy even lower prices. The phenomenon of export disorder has led to price wars among clustered firms for export orders (Wang *et al.*, 2007).

Developed countries have controlled the distribution channels of most industrial clusters and can enjoy cost advantages through R&D, design, branding and so on. At present, many clustered firms in China are producing through OEM and profit margins are low. International trade frictions on Chinese textile and clothing products have been on the rise since the accession to the WTO. In the post-quota era, textile and clothing clusters in China are facing challenges including the new forms of trade protectionism and the upgrading of industry under the global financial crisis. The textile and clothing firms in the cluster not only need to get used to new trade rules but also deal with fierce competition in terms of product, pricing and technology.

Under the more recent liberal trade regime in the global textile and clothing industry, fiercer domestic competition has the potential to harm the continued development and overall interests of textile and clothing industrial clusters in China. For example, Japan filed a series of anti-dumping allegations against Chinese towels at the beginning of 2000. The investigation indicated that 40% of towels exported to Japan had been made by Japanese firms in China. The industrial association in Japan intended to attack their Chinese counterparts adopting a low-price strategy through anti-dumping allegations so as to protect the interests of Japanese firms. In order to maintain the normal order of Chinese firms exporting towels to Japan, the Chinese Textile Import and Export Chamber of Commerce successfully organized the producers and suppliers in China, in reaching an agreement on the certification of Chinese firms exporting towels to Japan. The towels exported to Japan by Chinese towel suppliers were released by customs according to the approval documents issued by the Chinese Textile Import and Export Chamber of Commerce. The policy eventually prevented chaos associated with Chinese firms exporting towels to Japan and promoted the development of the towel industry in China (Bureau of Fair Trade for Imports and Exports, 2006).

China, the world's largest producer and exporter of textiles and clothing, accounts for one-fifth of the world's total production. According to China National Textile & Clothing Council (CNTAC), 133 textile and clothing clusters were developed in 57 cities and 74 towns in China in 2007, mainly located in the coastal provinces, including Zhejiang, Jiangsu, Guangdong, Fujian, Shandong and Hebei (see Table 3.9). Two-thirds of the textile clusters are located in Zhejiang and Jiangsu provinces while one-third of the clothing clusters are located in Guangdong province, and one-fifth in Zhejiang Province (CNTAC, 2007b).

Both Zhejiang and Jiangsu provinces are located in the Yangtze River Delta and their economic integration has been further strengthened in the new century. The "Wenzhou model" and the "Sunan model" converged gradually at the end of the 1990s. The development of textile and clothing clusters in Jiangsu province follows the same route as those in Ningbo City and Shaoxing City of Zhejiang province. The textile and clothing industry in Guangdong province has been mainly driven by foreign direct investment after China adopted its open-door policy. In particular, many companies in Hong Kong have shifted their operations to Guangdong in the past two decades to make use of the cheaper production and labor costs. However, as the textile and clothing clusters in China have become one of the main sourcing bases for textile and clothing that are sold in the global market, the industrial clusters have also become more export-oriented and participated in Original Equipment Manufacturer (OEM) actively. Therefore, the textile and clothing clusters in Zhejiang province are typical of such clusters in China and suitable for the case studies in the research.

In recent years, the textile and clothing clusters in China have been trying to extend the vertical value chain, coordinate cluster development with local commodity trading markets and make spatial expansion home

Table 3.9.   The major textile and clothing clusters in China.

Province	Cities/Counties/ Towns	Products
Zhejiang Province	Ningbo City	Men's and women's leisurewear, children's wear, and knitted garments.
	Shaoxing City	Light textiles, men's and women's leisurewear.
	Yiwu City	Socks, non-woven clothings.
	Pinghu City	Work suits, leisure wear, cotton jackets, artificial leather wear, raincoats, knitwear, women's wear and down clothing mainly for exports.
	Shengzhou City	Neckties
	Zhili Town	Children's wear
	Tatan Town	Socks
Jiangsu Province	Wujiang City	Synthetic fiber, men's, women's, leisurewear, and silk products.
	Changshu City	Leisurewear, knitted sweater, feather and down.
	Jintan City	Men's, women's, leisurewear mainly for exports.
Guangdong Province	Xiqiao City	Light textile, textile materials and clothing accessories.
	Shaxi Town	Leisurewear
	Xintang	Denim wear

Source: National Textile & Clothing Council (2007).

and abroad to meet the fierce international competition and combat against global financial turmoil.

3.4.1. *Making the extension of vertical value chain*

In China, most textile and clothing firms are still engaged in low value-added processing activities. Their business scope has expanded as the firms have developed. Consequently, some firms have engaged in the strategy of vertical integration. More relevant activities come into play and cover nearly all stages of the value chain, ranging from producing textile fabrics to processing ready-to-wear garments and marketing the final products to consumers. The clusters are also able to create their own brands and enjoy higher profit margins (Li & Fung Research Centre, 2006a).

3.4.2. *Coordinated cluster development with local commodity trading markets*

The commodity trading markets act as major marketing and distribution channels for the large quantity of textile materials and products manufactured in the cluster. The markets supply more and more mid-range branded clothes and some franchised fashion stores have also been opened within the market.

According to the *Statistical Yearbook of China Commodity Exchange Market in 2005*, there were 409 textile and clothing commodity exchange markets with an annual turnover above RMB100 million in China. The number of booths hit 475,842 units and the total turnover reached RMB473.17 billion in 2005, among which the wholesale business accounted for RMB418.54 billion while the retailing sector earned RMB54.62 billion. Table 3.10 lists the Top 20 textile and clothing trading markets in China in 2005. The commodity trading markets serve as a platform for small textile and clothing firms to be informed of market trends, lowering information costs because they usually do not have large information networks. In addition, they offer a series of supporting services for trading and sourcing textile and clothing products, including logistics, exhibition, finance and translation. The commodity trading markets have helped the SMEs to connect all parts of the value chain so that locally produced textiles and clothing can be marketed easily at home and abroad.

3.4.3. *Making spatial expansion home and abroad*

The clustered textile and clothing firms in China have extended their cross-regional and cross-border business activities in recent years so as to establish their own marketing networks. With further economic

Table 3.10.   The Top 20 textile and clothing trading markets in China in 2005.

Name of textile and clothing trading markets	Province	Turnover (RMB billion)
Shaoxing China Light Textile City	Zhejiang	25.82
Wujiang China Eastern Silk Market	Jiangsu	25.03
Haicheng Xiliu Clothing Market	Liaoning	19.20
Xiqiao Light Textile City	Guangdong	16.97
Shaoxing Qianqing Light Textile Raw Material Market	Zhejiang	15.06
Changshu Commercial Town	Jiangsu	12.00
Zhili Children's Wear Market	Zhejiang	10.54
Dieshiqiao Embroidery Market	Zhejiang	10.00
Datang Light Textile and Socks City	Zhejiang	9.34
Zichuan Clothing City	Shangdong	7.42
Jimo Garment Wholesale Market	Shangdong	6.96
Changshu Textile Commodity Exchange Market	Jiangsu	6.12
Hangzhou Sijiqing Clothing Market	Zhejiang	6.07
Shaoxing Yuezhou Light Textile Industrial Park	Zhejiang	6.01
Haining China Leather City	Zhejiang	5.69
Chuangang Bed Lining Products Market	Jiangsu	4.00
Tongxiang Fuyuan Woollen Sweater Market	Zhejiang	3.59
Haining China Textile City	Zhejiang	3.50
Liucheng Xiangjiang Market	Shandong	3.23
Tangshan Lunan District Xiaoshan Industrial Products Trading Market	Hebei	2.84

Source: National Bureau of Statistics of China (2006).

integration in the Yangtze River Delta, business expansion into Shanghai has become a trend for clustered firms in Zhejiang province. Shanghai is the economic center of China, accumulating capital, technology and talents. Some clustered firms make use of this platform to establish national and international marketing networks after they set up exclusive shops in the downtown area while others move their headquarters to Shanghai to gather the latest information and make better capital management. The rapid expansion of clothing clusters in Guangdong province is partly attributed to the extensive trade networks in Hong Kong. Their proximity to internationally metropolitan Shanghai and Hong Kong enables the textile and clothing clusters to market their products to the world market efficiently. Most textile and clothing clusters are located in coastal regions and they take advantage of the major logistic infrastructure there to distribute imported finished textile products and fabric from other countries. For instance, Humen Town in Dongguan City, Guangdong province has a well-developed port, which facilitated its industrial exports greatly and contributed considerably to the development of the textile and clothing industry in the region, making it renowned as the "No. 1 Fashion Wholesaler in China" (Li & Fung Research Centre, 2006b).

At the same time, the textile and clothing firms in China are making spatial expansion to the Asia-Pacific LDCs because of the overcapacity within the domestic market, the increasing international trade frictions on Chinese textile and clothing exports, the adjustment of domestic industrial policy and tax policy and the implementation of "Go Global" strategy by the Chinese government.

3.4.3.1. *The overcapacity within the domestic market*

The textile and clothing industry in China has formed strong competitive advantages in the past two decades. China has become the world's biggest textile and clothing producer and exporter. Its synthetic fiber output accounts for one-third of the whole world. The production capacity in the textile and clothing sector has expanded so dramatically that the domestic market finds it difficult to accommodate. The OFDI of textile and clothing enterprises in China can help to ease the excessive domestic production capacity and promote the structural adjustment and industrial upgrading (Wang *et al.*, 2009).

3.4.3.2. *The increasing international trade frictions on Chinese textile and clothing exports*

Due to the increasing international trade frictions on Chinese textile and clothing exports from both developed and developing countries, the Ministry of Commerce in China issued *Provisional Measures for the Administration of Textiles Exports* on 18 September 2005. Under these measures, The Ministry of Commerce, the General Administration of Customs, and the General Administration for Quality Supervision, Inspection and Quarantine (AQSIQ) compiled a *Catalogue of Textiles Products Subject to Interim Export Administration*, which lists textiles and clothing exports subject to restrictions imposed by countries or regions unilaterally, and those subject to temporary quantitative control under bilateral agreements (WTO, 2008). A new quota allocation system was applied to textiles and clothing exporters. The textile and clothing quotas, which are subject to an annual review, were allocated at lower prices by adopting various means of invitation for bid. Meanwhile, the quotas were allowed to be transferred by agreement in 2007.

China and EU have also reached a new agreement on textiles and clothing trade. Since 1 January 2008, all the textile and clothing exports from China to EU have not been subject to any quota or quantity cap. However, both parties agreed to implement a "Dual Approval and Supervisory System". China has imposed export license system on eight types of textile products including T-Shirts, pullovers, trousers, blouses, sheets, dresses, brassieres and linen shirts while EU has implemented a voluntary import license system (EU, 2008).

However, the LDCs in the Asia-Pacific region can still enjoy the preferential access to the US and EU markets. The US imposed quota restrictions on about 30 categories of ready-made garments (RMG) exports from Bangladesh, which are much less than those from China. The foreign RMG enterprises in Bangladesh can obtain Certificate of Origin easily if they make use of over 70% local fabrics. The European importers can have 13.5% tax redemption if the textile products have Certificate of Origin from Bangladesh (The State Council, 2007).

3.4.3.3. *The adjustment of domestic industrial policy and tax policy*

Chinese textile and clothing firms not only need to meet new trade rules but also confront fiercer competition from other developing countries in terms of product, pricing and technology. The sustainable development and overall interests of textile and clothing firms might be harmed if they fail to make industrial adjustment and technological innovation. Currently, the technological innovation is still limited in the textile and clothing industry and the ratio of R&D expenditure to total sales is less than 1%. The textile and clothing firms need to establish their own original famous brands in the international market.

On 23 July 2007, the Chinese government also issued *"Catalogue of Commodity under the Restricted Categories in Processing Trade"*, which listed 1,853 types of restricted commodities in processing trade including textiles (excluding clothing), furniture and so on. The Ministry of Commerce and General Administration of Customs amended the catalog on 1 February 2009 (KPMG, 2009). These policies aim to reduce the widening trade surplus and promote the domestic industrial adjustment. The government will further take measures to restrict the high energy-consumption and high-pollution resource-based exports, encourage exports with indigenous intellectual property rights and expand the domestic demand. China is moving from the manufacturing of labor-intensive products such as textiles and clothing products to more capital-intensive products such as electronics in the coming decades. For example, the Yangtze River Delta has still maintained its high growth of national exports because of shifting to more capital-intensive industries. The global credit crunch has accelerated the industrial transformation in China.

The adjustment of tax policy has further reduced the corporate profits in China. The Chinese government has started to implement a new corporate income tax law since 1 January 2008. According to *Notice on Implementation Measures on Transitional Policy of Preferential Corporate Income Tax*, all the enterprises including the SMEs that previously enjoyed a preferential tax rate will transit to the statutory tax rate gradually in the following five years. The enterprises enjoying a 15% corporate income tax rate are subject to a new tax rate of 18%, 20%, 22%, 24% and 25% in 2008, 2009, 2010, 2011 and 2012 respectively while those enterprises with an existing 24% tax rate are subject to a tax rate of 25% from 2008 (Wang *et al.*, 2009).

3.4.3.4. *"Go Global" strategy by the Chinese government*

The Chinese government has been encouraging and supporting textile and clothing firms to go global with a series of promotion policies. In

2005, the Ministry of Finance and the Ministry of Commerce jointly issued *Circular on Administrative Measures on Special Fund for Foreign Economic and Technological cooperation* ([2005] No. 255) to subsidize the earlier stage expenses of enterprises undertaking foreign economic and technological cooperation such as the expenditure on composing the project feasibility report, technological and consultancy fee, subsidy for loan interest without exceeding five years and overseas business expense. According to Zhejiang province's *Measures on the Administration of the Fund to Support Companies to "Go Global"* on 7 December 2005, the fund is to support the establishment of overseas specialized wholesale markets, the manufacturing enterprises and R&D institutions, the implementation of "market diversification" strategy, the promotion of overseas marketing by small- and medium-sized enterprises and the participation in overseas trade and investment fair by the enterprises (Zhejiang Foreign Trade and Economic Cooperation Bureau, 2007).

On 26 July 2006, a Special Fund was set up to support the restructuring of the textiles industry and the efforts of Chinese textile companies to "Go Global". The Ministry of Finance, the State Development and Reform Commission and the Ministry of Commerce issued *Circular on Relevant Policies to Promote Chinese Textile Industry to Shift New Ways of Growth in Foreign Trade and Support Chinese Textile Enterprises to Go Global*, allocating a special government fund amounting to RMB1.36 billion to encourage technology innovation, industrial upgrading and overseas direct investment by textile enterprises. In particular, the government supports the establishment of overseas economic and trade zones by granting subsidies for loan interest, land supply, manufacturing facilities, infrastructure and supporting services. The initial scale of fund reached RMB560 million, which was appropriated to provincial governments that were required to formulate their own measures on the administration of the fund in accordance with the guidelines set by the central government. The amount of the fund received by each province varies proportionately with exports and over seas investment of that province (WTO, 2008). For example, Jiangsu province issued *Measures on the Administration of the Fund to Support Companies to Go Global* on 26 October 2006, allocating the fund to support the establishment of overseas economic and trade zones, overseas direct investment by textile companies, set-up of overseas marketing and sales network and activities of service companies in facilitating overseas investment of textile companies (JSDOFTEC, 2006).

The establishment of overseas economic and trade zones has been actively promoted by the Chinese government. Ministry of Commerce hopes that the industries with domestic competitive advantages and massive production capability such as textiles, clothing, electronic appliances, construction materials, non-ferrous metal and processing of agricultural products will be transferred gradually to overseas economic and trade zones so as to avoid trade frictions and establish international marketing network. Around 16 overeas economic and trade zones have been established in 13 countries including Cambodia, Vietnam, Thailand, Indonesia, Nigeria, Egypt, and Zambia (Xinhua News, 2011, 2012). They are mainly attracting Chinese enterprises including the SMEs. Most of these economic and trade zones have completed infrastructure construction for the entry of enterprises and they are serving as one of the important platforms for the OFDI of domestic textile and clothing firms in China. In addition, the Ministry of Commerce has been sponsoring a series of foreign economic and trade fairs to promote the overseas economic and trade zones since the beginning of 2008 (Wang *et al.*, 2009).

3.5. Conclusion

The textile and clothing industry has played an important role in the industrialization of China. In the past three decades, the textile and clothing industry in China has successfully attracted substantial FDI and is currently highly export-oriented. It has become an important pillar for earning foreign exchange over the years.

Until the mid-1980s, the textile and clothing industry was wholly state-owned, and was the largest such industry in the world in terms of total output and production capacity. However, by the mid-1990s, the state-owned textile enterprises were suffering from huge losses. The textile industry was chosen as the first state-owned sector for industrial restructuring, which led to the emergence and development of the textile and clothing clusters in China. Under the Ninth Five-Year Plan in 1996, both central and local governments began to promote the necessary structural adjustments to restore the industry's competitiveness and upgrade the industrial sector. Since China's accession to the WTO in 2001, the central government has taken a series of measures including reducing the tax rebates for low value-added textile exports, limiting the investment of 28 types of mainly low grade and highly polluting textiles, protecting intellectual property rights and upgrading labor skills in order to adjust the industrial structure and meet fiercer international competition. With the rapid growth of the textile and clothing industrial clusters, the local government abandoned its traditional viewpoint of regional protectionism by encouraging economic integration of different regions thereby creating a sound industrial and trade environment.

One of the important phenomena of recent economic globalization has been the large-scale relocation of certain production processes to developing countries. Though the textile and clothing clusters in China can still take advantage of cheap land and low-cost labor, labor costs are nonetheless on the rise while at the same time clustered firms have to deal with more and more anti-dumping allegations as part of the globalization process. The sustainable development of textile and clothing clusters therefore needs to rely more and more on making indigenous innovations, upgrading production technology, strengthening industrial coordination and encouraging integration into the global value chain. Multinational firms in developed countries usually do not want to break up the entire value chain despite constant international institutional change and some may well help protect the interests of Chinese firms by lobbying their governments to remove trade protection. The textile and clothing clusters in China need to continue to extend the value chain, strengthen inter-firm linkages, create famous regional brands, establish a platform for professional services and promote the development of industrial associations.

The state has been playing a significant role in the recent development of textile and clothing clusters in China. After the restructuring of state-owned textile enterprises at the end of 1990s, the state-owned textile companies were placed on the same footing as private and foreign-invested firms. While the state-owned textile industry has steadily declined in relative terms since then, however, state intervention has played — and continues to play — a critical role in the development and upgrading of Chinese textile and clothing clusters. However, the public–private interface has taken a new form. The following chapters will examine the public–private interface from the perspectives of informal and formal institutions to reflect an on-going symbiotic relationship between the state and business in the context of global institutional change.

4

INSTITUTIONAL CHANGE AND THE DEVELOPMENT OF INDUSTRIAL CLUSTERS IN ZHEJIANG PROVINCE

4.1. Introduction

The rapid regional development in Zhejiang Province ("Zhejiang model") has aroused great attention in the academic circle in the past decades (Parris, 1993; Shi *et al.*, 2002; Huang and Di, 2004; Bellandi and Lombardi, 2012). Zhejiang model is partly traced back to the "Wenzhou model". However, some local governments in the northern part of Zhejiang Province also exhibited the features of Southern Jiangsu model in the 1980s. But they started to emulate the Wenzhou model and implemented liberal economic policies in the early 1990s (Huang, 2005). Since the beginning of 1990s, distinct regional development trajectories have emerged in other cities in Zhejiang Province including View City, Shaoxing City and Taizhou City and so on. Zhejiang model has been influential in the regional development of China since its adoption of open door policy in 1978 (Zhou, 2011).

Zhejiang province is located in the southern part of the Yangtze River Delta on the southeast coast of China. It faces the East China Sea on the east and neighbor Fujian Province on the south. With an extensive hinterland in the rear, it shares borders with Jiangxi Province and Anhui Province on the west, and Shanghai City and Jiangsu Province on the north (see Fig. 4.1). This chapter gives an overview of the development of industrial clusters in Zhejiang Province and explores the role of informal and formal institutions in the formation and development of SMEs industrial clusters there.

Fig. 4.1.   The map of Zhejiang Province, the People's Republic of China.

Source: Available at http://www.zj.gov.cn/zjforeign/english/node493/node499/index.html.

Informal institutions such as social networks, rural entrepreneurial mentality and political capital have been the foundation for the formation and development of SME industrial clusters in rural Zhejiang province. Zhejiang Province enjoyed the institutional first-mover advantages of regional deregulation under Chinese style federalism in the 1980s (Montinola *et al.*, 1995; Blanchard and Shleifer, 2001; Zhou, 2012). The local government were empowered to take part in the regional development as planners, reformers, and developers (Wei, 2002). The local state in Zhejiang Province possesses the features of both developmental state and liberal regulatory state to undertake a series of formal institutional innovation, thereby promoting rural industrialization. As a consequence, the rural entrepreneurship developed rapidly in the province in spite of a less favorable national institutional environment because the local state encouraged free markets and removed predatory and discriminatory regulatory policies (Zhou, 2011).

4.2. The Development of Industrial Clusters in Zhejiang Province

The economy of Zhejiang province has witnessed rapid development in the past three decades. From 1978 to 2011, the GDP rose from RMB12.4 billion to RMB3,231.885 billion, ranking fourth among all the provinces in China after Guangdong, Jiangsu and Shandong provinces. In 2011, the total industrial added-value reached RMB1,087.8 billion and increased by 10.9%. The state-owned and state-holding industrial enterprises realized RMB194.6 billion, rising by 9.6% while the private industrial enterprises realized RMB428.3 billion, increasing by 12.3% (see Table 4.1).

The development of private economy in Zhejiang Province started at the beginning of 1980s. By the end of 2008, there were 408,000 privately controlled enterprises, accounting for 90.6% of all enterprises. The number of employees reached 14.523 million, accounting for 77.9% of all enterprises (see Table 4.2). The private controlling enterprises are mainly located in Hangzhou, Ningbo and Wenzhou regions. They are mainly engaged in the secondary industries such as manufacturing industry, wholesale and retail industry. As Table 4.3 indicates, the manufacturing industry mainly covers textile, plasticware, metal products, general-purpose equipment manufacturing

Table 4.1. The added-value of large-scale industrial enterprises in Zhejiang Province in 2011.

	Absolute value (RMB billion)	Growth rate over the previous year (%)
Industrial added-value	1087.8	10.9
State-owned and state-holding enterprises	194.6	9.6
Limited liability enterprises	174.4	10.6
Shareholding enterprises	95.2	11.9
Investment enterprises by foreign businessmen or those from Taiwan, Hong Kong and Macau	286.8	9.0
Private enterprises	428.3	12.3
Light industry	449.8	10.0
Heavy industry	638	11.5

Source: Zhejiang Provincial Bureau of Statistics (2012a).

and electromechanical equipment manufacturing (Zhejiang Provincial Bureau of Statistics, 2011).

4.2.1. *Widespread SME industrial clusters in rural area*

Zhejiang Province has been well known for "petty commodities, large market, one commodity each town, one industry each county" in China since the 1980s (Sonobe *et al.*, 2004; Wei *et al.*, 2007; Wang, 2011). The scale of private enterprises in Zhejiang province is relatively small. However, when a large number of SMEs agglomerate and produce the same type or the same category of relative products together, industrial clusters have come into being. The agglomeration economy accounts for over 50% of total provincial output. In 2009, the sales of 82 industrial clusters exceeded RMB1 billion in the 90 counties, cities or townships (see Table 4.3).

Three industrial belts have been developed in Zhejiang province, including areas around Hangzhou Bay (six prefectural level cities, including Hangzhou City, Ningbo City, Jiaxing City, Shaoxing City, Zhoushan City and Huzhou City), Wen-Tai Coastland (Wenzhou City and Taizhou City), and areas along Jinhua-Quzhou-Lishui Highway (the area along the

Table 4.2. An overview of different types of holding enterprises in Zhejiang Province in 2008.

	Number of impersonal entity (10,000 units)	Ratio (%)	Number of employees (10,000 persons)	Ratio (%)	Operating income in the year (RMB100 million)	Ratio (%)	Total assets of enterprises (RMB100 million)	Ratio (%)
Total	45.1	100.0	1865.1	100.0	81199	100.0	89811	100.0
State controlling	1.0	2.2	125.4	6.7	12627	15.6	21760	24.2
Collective holding	1.6	3.6	71.3	3.8	2943	3.6	4211	4.7
Private holding	40.8	90.6	1452.3	77.9	53680	66.1	49773	55.4
Hong Kong, Macao and Taiwan businessmen holding	0.6	1.2	78.0	4.2	3618	4.5	4643	5.2
Foreign investment holding	0.7	1.5	85.7	4.6	4760	5.9	5298	5.9
Others	0.4	0.9	52.4	2.8	3571	4.4	4125	4.6

Source: Zhejiang Provincial Bureau of Statistics (2012b).

Table 4.3.   The three industrial belts and main SME industrial clusters in Zhejiang Province.

	Cities	Major industries	Typical industrial clusters
Area around Hangzhou Bay	Hangzhou City	Textiles and clothing (e.g., silk, dyeing), electronic information, large-scale machinery and equipment.	Ladies' wear in the urban area of Hangzhou City and synthetic fibers in Xiaoshan district.
	Ningbo City	Clothing, machinery, and petrochemicals.	Clothing in Yinzhou District and moulds in Yuyao City.
	Shaoxing City	Textiles and clothing, chemical for dyeing.	China Textile City in Shaoxing county and neckties in Shenzhou city.
	Jiaxing City	Textiles, leather, toys, machinery and instruments.	Woollen knitted sweaters in Tongxiang City, leather and warp knitting in Haining City, clothing and suitcases in Pinghu City, and silk products in Xiuzhou district, Jiaxing City.
	Huzhou City	Textile and clothing (e.g., silk, dyeing, children's wear), building materials.	Children's wear in Zhili Town, building materials in Nanxun Town, and bamboo products in Anji County.
	Zhoushan City	Processing of aquatic products, aquatic medicine, and machinery.	

(Continued)

Table 4.3. (*Continued*)

Cities	Major industries	Typical industrial clusters
Area Along Jinhua-Quzhou-Lishui Highway Wenzhou City	Glasses, lighters, shoes, buttons, and low-voltage electric appliances.	Glasses, lighters, shoes in the urban area of Wenzhou City, buttons in Yongjia County, and low-voltage electric appliances in Yueqing City.
Taizhou City	Plastic products, auto parts.	Plastic products in Jiaojiang City.
Central and south-western region Jinhua City	Textiles, socks, hardware, jewellery and ornaments.	Yiwu China Commodity City and hardware in Yongkang City.
Quzhou City	Fertilizer, cement, and mechanical electric appliances.	
Lishui City	Wood processing, handicrafts, shoes, toys, and umbrellas.	Umbrellas in Longquan City and wooden toys in Yunhe County.

Sources: Zhu (2003, pp. 56–57) and Zhejiang Provincial Bureau of Statistics (2011).

highway linking three prefectural level cities including Jinhua City, Quzhou City and Lishui City) (Zhejiang Provincial Bureau of Statistics, 2011).

4.2.2. *The interaction between SMEs and commodity trading market*

The commodity trading market is a specialized market and has offered a mechanism for making effective allocation of industrial resources and a wide marketing network for the local SMEs. The agglomeration of a large number of products within the commodity trading market has not only reduced the transaction costs considerably, but also sent the latest market and product information to the local SMEs, helping to improve their technology and productivity as well as promoting the flow of factors of production. In addition, the commodity trading market contributes to the building of regional brands and the reduction of corporate marketing expenditure (Zheng, 2000). By the end of 2011, there were 731 commodity trading markets with annual sales exceeding RMB100 million in Zhejiang province (see Table 4.4). The Top 10 commodity trading markets in Zhejiang province are China Yiwu Small Commodity City, Zhejiang Shaoxing China Textile City, Zhejiang China Science and Technology Hardware City, Yuyao China Plastic City, Qianqing China Light Textile Raw Material City, Hangzhou Canal Steel Market, Zhejiang New Century Metals Spot Market, Hangzhou North City Metals Market, Xiaoshan Commercial City and Shaoxing Yue Zhou Light Textile Industrial Park. The total transaction volume of these 10 specialized wholesale markets reached RMB37.7 billion in 2011. The scale of commodity trading market continues to expand. The market network has promoted the rapid growth of SMEs in the province (Zhejiang Provincial Bureau of Statistics, 2012c).

Table 4.4.   Distribution of commodity trading markets with gross turnover over RMB100 million in Zhejiang Province in 2011.

Area	Number of markets		Gross turnover	
	Number (Unit)	Ratio in the province (%)	Value (RMB million)	Ratio in the province (%)
Total	731	100	13100.5	100
Hangzhou City	172	23.5	3664.6	28.0
Ningbo City	131	17.9	2166.0	16.5
Wenzhou City	74	10.1	761.4	5.8
Jiaxing City	59	8.1	1130.3	8.6
Huzhou City	45	6.2	587.8	4.5
Shaoxing City	50	6.8	1957.0	14.9
Jinhua City	54	7.4	1564.9	12.0
Quzhou City	22	3.0	241.4	1.8
Zhoushan City	11	1.5	153.6	1.2
Taizhou City	97	13.3	733.6	5.6
Lishui City	16	2.2	139.9	1.1

Source: Zhejiang Provincial Bureau of Statistics (2012c),

4.2.3. *The rapid growth of economic development zones*

Zhejiang Provincial Government has invested substantially in the establishment of economic development zones to promote the industrial agglomeration. The inward FDI is highly concentrated in the state-level and provincial-level economic development zones, and export processing zones, which have promoted the rapid development of regional economy. By the end of 17 October 2012, state-level economic development zones had been approved by the State Council. About 50 provincial-level economic development zones and four export processing zones had been approved by Zhejiang Provincial Government. In 2011, a total of 640 foreign investment projects were carried out within the 64 state-level and provincial-level economic development zones with the actual use of foreign capital amounting to USD5.98 billion. More than 90,000 enterprises were put into operation. The total import and export volume reached USD131.5, accounting for 42.5% of that in Zhejiang province (Department of Commerce of Zhejiang Province, 2012).

The state-level and provincial-level development zones and export processing zones have contributed substantially to the promotion of regional economic development, structural adjustment and industrial upgrading in Zhejiang province. For example, as a state-level economic development zone, Hangzhou Economic and Technological Development Area (HETDA) has witnessed the establishment of 474 foreign-funded enterprises from 39 countries and regions with a total contracted investment volume of USD5.808 billion since 1993. 23 out of Top 500 multinational enterprises have launched 49 projects within the economic development zone. The strategic objectives of HETDA were to build it into a sub-center of Hangzhou City engaging in the development of secondary industry in the eastern part of Hangzhou City in 1998. With the rapid economic and social development, they have been adjusted to develop HETDA into an ecological garden-like modern urban area incorporating business services, high technology, advanced manufacturing industry and high education. Up to now, HETDA has developed the following significant industries including food and beverage, electronic information, biological pharmaceuticals, mechanical manufacturing (automobile parts and components), household electrical appliances.

Meanwhile, two functional zones have been introduced to HETDA including Hangzhou Xiasha Higher Education Zone and Zhejiang Export Processing Zone (Li, 2009).

The economic development zones have offered a better platform for promoting the professional inter-firm cooperation among the agglomerated enterprises. Many development zones have tried to create a regionally innovative environment to promote technological progress. Meanwhile, the economic development zones provide an attractive investment environment. For instance, the relevant departments of local government have established their offices in the economic development zones to provide a full-range of services regarding the examination, approval, construction and operation of the enterprises in the zones. The foreign-invested enterprises in the economic development zones can also enjoy certain preferential treatment with regard to taxation and the use of land (Department of Commerce of Zhejiang Province, 2012).

The fierce market competition has accelerated the transition of some private enterprises from labor-intensive industries to high-tech industries. Hi-tech industrial parks have also been established throughout the province. The Yingzhou District of Ningbo City has been well-known for the clothing industry. At the beginning of 2000s, the local government started to adopt a strategy of transforming the traditional industries into high-tech industries and industrial application of new and high technologies. Some clothing firms have diversified their businesses and entered into the high-tech industry, including IT, electronics, biomedicine, petrochemicals, new materials and new energy. For example, Shanshan Group, one of leading clothing firms, established Shanshan Science and Technology Park in Yinzhou district in March 2005. Shanshan Technology Group 800T/Y anode material project for lithium-ion battery is the first national high-tech industrialized demonstration project in Ningbo City. The group has forged strategic alliances with some leading research institutes affiliated with China Scientific Academy, Zhejiang University, Shanghai Jiao Tong University, Harbin Industrial University and Yamagata University in Japan (Ningbo Yinzhou District Science and Technology Bureau, 2008). The new high-tech firms have continued to be attracted to the industrial parks. Currently, there are 163 state-level high-tech enterprises in Yinzhou district. The incubation area in the district covers about 80,000 square meters with 165 incubating high-tech enterprises. In 2009, the output of high-tech products in the district amounted to RMB78 billion. The rapid growth of high-tech enterprises have not only promoted regional development, but also improved the innovative capability in the region (Xu *et al.*, 2012).

4.2.4. *The spatial expansion of industrial clusters home and abroad*

The clustered firms in Zhejiang province have extended the cross-regional and cross-border business activities to establish their own marketing networks since the mid-1990s. With the relational intergenerational, and structural lock-ins, the clustered firms in Wenzhou region have gone through localization and delocalization. The establishment of new firms and clusters has been coupled with merge and acquisition, leading to the formation of multiregional enterprises, some of which have relocated their headquarters and specialized functions to metropolitan areas, particularly Shanghai City and Hangzhou City (Wei *et al.*, 2007). For example, in Liushi electrical equipment cluster of Wenzhou City, CHINT Group and Delixi Group, the leading industrial groups of low-voltage electrical equipment began to pursue vertical integration strategy from 1994 to 1996. CHINT Group, which was founded in July 1984, has expanded from a home workshop of seven workers to be one of the leaders in Chinese industrial electrical equipment production and clean energy fields. Its business has ranged from low-voltage electrical products to power transmission and distribution equipements and services, instruments and meters, buliding appliances, automobile parts, industrial automation, PV power generation, equipment manufacturing. It has also become the largest clean energy supplies and energy efficiency management solution provider with the most complete product ranges in China. It has established a sound global marketing network with its subsidiaries in Italy, Russia, Brazil, the United States and the United Arab Emirates and so on (CHINT Group, 2013).

Delixi Group develops from Yueqing Qiujing Switch Factory, which is a small workshop, established in July 1984, into one of the largest private firms in China specialized in the manufacturing of the electric power transmission and distribution appliances. It products a full range of high and low voltage switch gear sets, along with about 300 series of components in about 30,000 specifications. Since 1998, it has adopted a diversification strategy of integrating manufacturing and capital management. Shanghai Delixi Group Co., Ltd. which was established in 1998, primarily produces a series of low-, medium- and high-voltage electrical apparatus in cooperation with Xi'an High Voltage Electronics Research Institute. The group acquired the state-owned Hangzhou Xizi Group in 1999 and participated in the *"Developing the West"* initiative advocated by the central government in 2000 and restructured several state-owned enterprises in Xinjiang Uygur Autonomous Region and making investment to construct the Xinjiang De Hui International Plaza Mean while, it has internationalized its business in more than 40 countries (Delixi Group, 2013). CHINT Group and Delixi Group are two typical clustered firms making spatial expansion in the restructuring of "Wenzhou model" (Wei *et al.*, 2007). The SMEs in Haining leather cluster, YongKang hardware cluster, Shaoxing textile cluster and yiaru socks cluster have made domestic and overseas expansion with migrant entrepreneurs and internationalization of local commodity trading markets (Bellandi and Lombardi, 2012; Wang and Ngoasong, 2012).

4.3. Informal Institutions and the Development of Industrial Cluster in Zhejiang Province

The informal institutions embedded in Zhejiang province have contributed to the rapid development of SME industrial clusters. The entrepreneurial mentality of rural farmers embedded in traditional culture, is usually called the "Zhejiang Spirit", which is "independence, seeking benefit, exploitation and innovation, struggling for progress, and changing according to the reality" (Bellandi and Lombardi, 2012, p. 630). Social network is one of the typical informal institutions that has led to the formation and growth of SMEs in the region. According to Hakansson and Johanson (1993, p. 38), "Networking is all about finding people who have mutual advantage in co-operating". The actors in networks can be individuals, teams and organizations. Social networks in China traditionally rely on the importance of *Guanxi*, which is distinctively different from a traditional Western network in its approach.

Guanxi is identified as a connection in terms of social relationships such as family, relative, friends, business partners, and government officials. It can help people meet, bond and even maintain business relationship. Whereas a traditional network illustrates which individuals perform which tasks, *Guanxi* provides the ability to ask for a favor of those contacts within the network. The rules of social network, which have evolved through the long-term social interaction, have been infiltrated with the local culture. Confucianism is present in the everyday life of China. It advocates establishing social harmony with a hierarchical social order. The five cardinal human relationships that Confucianism defends include sincerity between father and son, righteousness between ruler and subjects, distinction or separate functions between husband and wife, and faithfulness among friends (Chen, 2005).

Face and *renqing*, the typical Chinese communication traits, are deeply linked to *Guanxi* in a manner that they will help one to cultivate and develop its network. *Face* helps people to maintain correct relationships by protecting someone's "face" or dignity. *Renqing* or "humanized obligations" involves social exchanges and obliges people to keep equity in mind. If one fails to follow the rule of equity in exchange of *renqing*, one loses his or her face, hurts the feelings of his or her friends and looks morally bad, and the social network will be in danger (Chen, 2005).

The SMEs industrial clusters in Zhejiang province are open networked organizations. The inter-firm network is more flexible and effective than the hierarchical large-scale enterprises. Network efficiency depends on the trust and cooperation among networked firms. Network forms of exchange entail indefinite, sequential transactions within the context of a general pattern of interaction. Sanctions are typically normative rather than legal. In hierarchies, communication occurs in the context of the employment contract. Relationships matter and the previous interactions shape current ones, but the patterns and context of intra-organizational exchange are most strongly shaped by one's position within the formal hierarchical structure of authority. However, under market transactions, the benefits to be exchanged are clearly specified and no trust is required. Agreements are bolstered by the power of legal sanction (see Table 4.5).

One of the main features of industrial clusters in Zhejiang province is that thousands of family workshops have promoted rural economic

Table 4.5. A stylized comparison among different forms of economic organizations.

Key features	Forms of economic organizations		
	Market	Hierarchy	Network
Normative basis	Contracts — property rights	Employment relationship	Complimentary strengths
Means of communication	Prices	Routines	Relational
Methods of conflict resolution	Haggling — resort to courts for enforcement	Administrative fiat — Supervision	Norm of reciprocity — Reputation concerns
Degree of Flexibility	High	Low	Medium
Amount of Commitment among the parties	Low	Medium to high	Medium to high
Tone of climate	Precision and/or suspicion	Formal, bureaucratic	Open-ended, mutual benefits
Actor preferences or choices	Independent	Dependent	Interdependent
Mixing of forms	Repeat transactions/ Contracts as hierarchical documents	Informal organization/ Market-like features: profit centers, transfer pricing	Status hierarchies, multiple partners and formal rules

Source: Powell (1990).

development. The family provides strong cohesion and family members enjoy cooperation and coordination on the basis of kinship. When the business is initially set up, family members usually do not care much about gains and losses of individuals. In addition, the business manager can bring into play his power and authority associated with his hierarchical relationships within the household. Power is usually concentrated while duties and responsibilities are clarified. The clustered firm, therefore, has the ability to react quickly (Zhu, 2003).

Without these SMEs, there would not be so many industrial clusters. They are not independent production systems, but production networks made up of SMEs with all kinds of social relationships including households, neighbors and friends. There is specialized division of labor within production networks. Strong ties within industrial networks have made these SMEs an efficient large-scale entity. Inter-firm networks have become essential for the survival and development of SMEs. Firstly, the division of labor reduces the capital threshold of new entrants and solves the bottleneck of capital shortage in rural areas. Secondly, since the division of labor has been based on relations on the basis of siblings, kinship or regional ties, the resulting low transaction costs among SMEs, the scattered operation risks and rapid information flows to do with technology and marketing have generated high collective efficiency and improvement in the competitiveness of the whole industrial cluster. Moreover, the SMEs within the industrial clusters have forged formal and informal horizontal and vertical linkages to produce intermediate and finished products. They forecast market trends, exchange production and management experiences together. However, with fiercer competition and constantly changing markets, these family businesses need to make prompt and efficient decisions to gain a secure foothold in the market (Zhu, 2003).

In the development of industrial clusters, social networks influence the formation of industrial networks, the diffusion of internal knowledge and information within industrial clusters and the performance of entrepreneurship (Zhang *et al.*, 2011). Since the mid- to late-1980s, a lot of entrepreneurs with extraordinary innovative spirits have become the main driving force of cluster formation and development. The entrepreneurs running the TVEs were the main force promoting the rural development in China in the 1980s (Oi, 1999). Today, it is private entrepreneurs who are promoting the development and upgrading of industrial clusters throughout the whole Zhejiang province.

Social networks have been an important and even critical resource for entrepreneurship in Zhejiang province because they are critical to the survival of private entrepreneurs and operating efficiency. In China, it is very important to take advantage of *Guanxi* to gain the market entry and obtain the loans from the state-owned banks, in particular during the previous planned economy and the early stage of economic transition (Zhou, 2011). The business activities depend much on bureaucracy. Those private entrepreneurs with special social status can establish successful business more easily. The wider their social network is, the more easily they can gain business opportunities and reduce business risks (Jacobs *et al.*, 2004).

The main reason why social networks perform these functions is that the rural areas in Zhejiang province were unable to obtain raw materials for industrial use through formal institutional arrangements in the previous planned economic system in the 1980s. The urban and rural economy was separated at that time (Wang, 2008). Besides, the natural resources in the rural areas of Zhejiang province were scarce and the information was incomplete. The previous industrial base was weak and there were great shortages of technology and capital. These factors hampered industrial development in the rural area of Zhejiang province (Wang and Shi, 2006). Therefore, entrepreneurs had to make use of social networks to establish relationships with economic and political organizations to gain information, capital, technology and raw materials, helping to expand their businesses and improve their capacities to sense commercial opportunities and potential threats. Even now, information asymmetry still exists in the transitional stage and social networks are still important for clustered firms to select and screen information (Zhou, 2011).

Another particular set of social networks exists in industrial clusters of Zhejiang Province, notably involving social connections between entrepreneurs and local government officials. The entrepreneur's participation in politics in China could be explained by the underdevelopment of markets and market-supporting institutions. The institutional environment influences the molivation of private entrepreneurs to take part in politics (Li *et al.*, 2006). Although the private economy has witnesses rapid development in the past decades and won the legitimate status, private entrepreneurs continue to rely on the Chinese state because the state controls the majority of essential resources (Yang, 2012). In some industrial clusters originating from the collective economy, certain political figures made huge gains for themselves as public assets were "privatized" during the transformation of the enterprise system in the 1990s. In China, one of the key factors in successful entrepreneurship is the ability to form an alliance with those economic agents who possess or control financial assets, physical assets, or specific human capital needed for brokering market entry, that is, for starting production, securing supply and gaining access to distribution channels in the economic transition in the 1980s. It is the same case even now. Such public–private alliances have helped firms to evade administrative entry barriers, reducing business risks and increasing their expected net returns (Krug and Mehta, 2004, p. 60). The folowing is a typical example reflecting the role of public–private alliance in the corporate growth.

Established in October 1994, Zhejiang Hengyi Group Co., Ltd. is currently a large business group specializing in Purified Terephthalic Acid (PTA), polyester spinning, chemical fiber, international trade and functional investemnt. With total assets of RMB20 billion, it was ranked 221th among Top 500 Enterprises in China in 2011 (Hengyi Group, 2012). The business group originates from a small TVE in late 1980s. Jianlin Qiu was invited to run Yaqian silk and Synthetic Fiber Cloth Factory by the local government in February 1989. It bacame one of the high-performing enterprises in the town with sales volume exceeding RMB10 million and profits surpassing RMB1 million in the following two years. In 1991, he was appointed Director of Xiaoshan Yarn Dyeing Factory, which was on the verge of bankruptcy. The enterprise was originally named Xiaoshan Yaqian knitting Factory. It was established by the local government in 1974 mainly for employing the intellectuals who had been sent down to the countryside. There were dozens of female workers with a few manual hosiery knitters in the factory. The main products were socks.

Jianlin Qiu was invited to run Yaqian Silk and Synthetic Fiber Cloth Factory by the local government in February 1989. It became one of the high-performing enterprises in the town with sales volume exceeding RMB10 million and profits surpassing RMB1 million in the following two years. In 1991, he was appointed Director of Xiaoshan Yarn Dyeing Factory, which was on the verge of bankruptcy. The enterprise was originally named Xiaoshan Yaqian Knitting Factory. It was established by the local government in 1974 mainly for employing the intellectuals who had been sent down to the countryside. There were dozens of female workers with a few manual hosiery knitters in the factory. The main products were socks.

Hengyi Group was established in 1991. Jianlin Qiu established Hengyi Dyeing Company and Hengyi Synthetic Fiber Company in 1992. In October 1994, Zhejiang Hengyi Group Co., Ltd. became the first provincial enterprise group in Zhejiang province after the implementation of *the Company Act*. It possesses an integrated production line of synthetic fiber, weaving and dyeing. It was transformed from a township enterprise into a private enterprise in 1997. In 1998, it became the first company to pass

ISO9002 quality certification in the local textile industry. In 1999, the group made an investment of RMB450 million to introduce the latest generation PET production line. The production capacity of polyester filaments subsequently reached 300,000 tons every year (Hengyi Group, 2012).

Before the mid-1990s, the investment management system in Xiaoshan district was mainly based on the planned economic model. All projects with an investment exceeding RMB50,000 had to be approved by the local government, whether state-owned, collective or private. The approval procedures, which consisted of registration of projects, evaluation of proposals and final approval, were complicated and time-consuming. The general managers had no authority to make decisions on human resources and the disposal of property. Gradually, other private firms in the region realized that they could make independent private investment decisions, so long as they conformed to the industrial policy and environmental standards without breaking the law.

Afterwards, many private enterprises in Zhejiang province broke through the policy restrictions and contributed to the dramatic increase of private capital and economic growth in the province, indicating that they had sufficient capacity and experience to enter into new business lines. In March 2003, the officials responsible for the management of social investment in the administrative area of Zhejiang province replaced the extant approval system with a new registration system.

In September 1999, Hengyi group made an investment of RMB450 million to build a new generation PET production line, which was one of the best-selling raw materials for the local textile industry. PET had been monopolized by the state-owned oil companies and joint ventures. In order to restrain the excessive investment in PET, the government issued a special announcement that all new polyester projects must have an approval certificate before being launched. All large-scale projects must have the approval of the State Council. No provincial government was allowed to approve PET projects and banks could not grant loans to them. Fully aware that the application for the PET project could not be approved, Hengyi Group made an application for producing agricultural plastic film, instead. The local government gave implied consent to the enterprise's decision because the enterprise was carrying out the strategy of extending the industrial chain. Otherwise, the further development of the textile industry would have been constrained by the lack of raw material.

The first enterprises to object to these decisions were the state-owned oil and chemical enterprises, Hengyi Group's competitors, which made complaints to the central government that the private investment of Hengyi group went against the state policy and harmed the interests of SOEs. The response from the central government was rapid and direct and a special team was set up to conduct the investigation. However, they were surprised to find that the production costs of Hengyi Group were much lower than those of the SOEs by adopting the latest technology. The inspectors from the central government did not stop the project. The second and third phases of the production line were thus put into operation with the tacit consent of the central government. The inspection team saw no reason why the local private enterprises should not be allowed to compete against the SOEs and joint ventures, which had been enjoying more privileges. The private enterprises could also produce high-quality PET products at a lower cost by introducing more advanced machinery and equipments.

When Hengyi group wanted to invest in its PTA project, it faced strict entry barriers. Under the approval system, the private enterprises in the cluster made use of their own capital, but they needed to have permission from the central government before launching the project. Although both the local and provincial governments had delegated their powers to the enterprises, some ministries of the state government still had some authority over approval for large-scale projects in China (Wu, 2004).

In the end, Zhejiang Hengyi Group and Zhejiang Rongsheng Chemical Fiber Group jointly invested to establish Zhejiang Yisheng Petrochemical Co., Ltd. in Beilun district, Ningbo City. The total investment reached RMB10 billion. The first PTA production line adopted the patented technology of the American INVITA Corporation. Kvaerner Engineering Company in the United Kingdom designed the infrastructure and the project was implemented by China Textile Industrial Engineering Institute. The project was launched on 22 May 2003. The PTA production line, which was worth RMB4.5 billion, was put into operation successfully on 18 March 2005, with an annual output of 530,000 tons (Li, 2007). Afterwards, the company continued to expand its PTA production capacity by establishing the large-scale PTA manufacturing subsidiaries in Dalian City, Shenyang Province in 2009 and in Yangpu economic development zone, Hainan Province in 2010. As a result, Hengyi Group becomes the largest PTA producer in China (Hengyi Petrochemical Co., Ltd, 2012).

In 2013, Hengyi Group obtained regulatory approval from State Development and Reform Committee of China and Burnei Government to bulid a planned US$4.32 billion refinery project in Burnei. The refinery complex will be able to produce 1.5 million tons of diesel, 400,000 tons of gasoline; 1 million tons of jet kerosene; 1.5 million tons of naphtha, 1.5 million tons of paraxylene (PX) and 500,000 tons of benzene annually. The project is designed to have steady supply of feedstocks PX and benzene for Hengyi Group's production of PTA, polyester and caprolactam, realizing the further vertical integration by cooperating with Brunei Shell Petroleum (Bakar and Begawan, 2013).

4.4. Institutional Innovation of the Local Government

The local government of Zhejiang Province has made a series of formal institutional innovation to promote the rapid development and internationalization of SME industrial clusters since the beginning of 1980s including the encouragement of private entrepreneurship, the formulation of industrial policy, the establishment of commodity trading markets and the implementation of "go out" strategy.

4.4.1. *Encouraging entrepreneurship and the development of private economy*

The formal institutional innovation by the local government has deeply affected the development path of industrial clusters in Zhejiang province. Institutional innovation in Zhejiang province was mainly induced from the grassroots at the first stage. In the 1980s, the Wenzhou model aroused substantial disputes within political circles in China and became one of the typical examples of bottom-up institutional innovation with the prosperity of family workshops and the emergence of shareholding cooperative system (Wei *et al.*, 2007). It is one of the typical examples of rural industrialization of China on the basis of internal markets, internal resources, and traditional manufacturing (Shi *et al.*, 2002). In Taizhou City, the local government also introduced Shareholding Cooperative system to promote the development of TVEs and private firms during the same period. With deepening specialized production and division of labor, some SME industrial clusters emerged including molding and plastic products (Qian and Shi, 2008).

The local government in Zhejiang province influenced grassroots institutional innovation mainly by the following means. First, the local governments in Zhejiang tolerated and encouraged private entrepreneurship and innovation even when those in other regions were suppressing it (Huang and Di, 2004). Second, the formulation of local administrative regulations and the legal acknowledgment of institutional innovation helped to create an atmosphere of encouraging entrepreneurship and innovation. Although the grassroots institutional innovations invigorated the rural economy, its potential for development was still limited. However, with the support of local government, institutional innovation was activated and diffused. The local government officials would make announcements after taking actions, strengthening the bargaining power between the lower-level and upper-level governments and increasing the possibility of reconstructing a new political and economic contract (Yang, 1998). The rapid development of SME industrial clusters in Zhejiang Province has been attributed to the institutional innovation induced by the private sector and formalized by the local government. Third, the local government officials made great efforts to private-sector institutions, especially local private financial institutions such as informal credit markets, to supply the essential factor resources to private firms, which were not easily accessible (Zhou, 2009, 2011; Ruan and Zhang, 2009).

Since the beginning of 1980s, Zhejiang Provincial Government has undertaken many important measures to ensure the development of private economy with formal institutions, which, in turn, promoted the emergence and growth of SME industrial clusters (see Table 4.6). The local government introduced a new management system for guiding rapid development of industrial clusters in Zhejiang province. The objective of reforming the administration system was to improve the regulation and efficiency of government to create a good environment for the development of local private economy (Zhu, 2003).

In the early stages of economic transition, institutional innovation was often interwoven with ideological issues. Consequently, the institutionalization of bottom-up institutional change in some parts of China was often

Table 4.6.   Formal institutions promoting the development of private economy in Zhejiang Province.

Time	Formal institutions
1981	The provincial government issued *Notice on Problems of Developing Various Forms of Business in Rural Area*, which required bringing the initiatives of individuals and collective enterprises to play.
1985	The provincial governor stated that the cadres at various levels and divisions discard prejudice and attach strategic importance to the development of household business and cooperative enterprises.
	The provincial congress issued *The Temporary Stipulations on Protecting the Legal Interests of Specialized Households in the Rural Areas of Zhejiang Province.*
1989	The provincial leaders stated that the reform of the experimental zone in Wenzhou had achieved great success.
1991	The provincial government issued *Notice on Strengthening the Management of Privately or Individually-owned Business and Private Enterprises in Urban or Rural Areas*, adopting the principle of "permitting coexistence, developing appropriately, promoting what is beneficial and abolishing what is harmful, strengthening guidance and management".
1992	The provincial committee stated at the Second Provincial Individual Workers' Delegates Conference and the First Provincial Delegates Conference that it be unnecessary to stick to the ratio of different forms of ownership. Privately- or individually-owned business and private enterprises must be encouraged to become the new driving force of local economic growth.
1993	The provincial government issued *Notice on Promoting the Healthy Development of Privately- or Individually-owned Business and Private Enterprises*, stating that privately- or individually-owned business and private enterprises can be engaged in any business except the industries and commodities that were prohibited by the national law.
1998	The provincial government issued *Notice on Developing the Non-Public Economy Vigorously*, determining to develop the privately- or individually-owned business vigorously and improve the quality of economic growth to create a fair and competitive environment for the non-public economy.
	The provincial committee declared clearly that the privately or individually owned business should be developed vigorously. The private entrepreneurs would be able to enjoy favorable economic treatment, political status and social honors.

(Continued)

Table 4.6. (*Continued*)

Time	Formal institutions
2000	The private entrepreneurs were awarded the status of "provincial model worker".
2005	*The provincial government issued measures on the Administration of the Fund to Support Companies to "Go Out".*
2008	*The provincial government issued notice on the Action Plan of Upgrading Indigenous Innovation Capability.*
2012	*The provincial government issued views on Upgrading Private Enterprises through Utilizing Foreign Capital.*
	Views on Further Promoting the Development of Commodity Trading Market, aiming to integrate market and industry, physical market and digital market further and realizing the annual trading volume of RMB2 trillion for physical and digital markets respectively.

Source: Fang *et al.* (2000) and the website of Zhejiang Provincial Development and Reform Commission (www.zjdpc.gov.cn).

at the cost of the political career of forward-looking local government officials. That such institutional innovation could be pushed gradually in Zhejiang province was due to the actions of these local elites, who had both innovative spirits and good educational backgrounds (Zhu, 2003).

4.4.2. *Building the commodity trading market*

Zhejiang Province has ranked the first in terms of the number of Commodity trading markets since 1993 (Li *et al.*, 2013). The commodity trading markets were mainly initiated by the rural farmers and entrepreneurs at the beginning of 1980s. However, in the late 1980s, the infrastructure of the extant commodity trading markets was unable to support the rapid development of SME industrial clusters, so the local government took an active part in the establishment of new-generation commodity trading markets. The local government officials were fully aware that the construction of commodity trading markets could promote the rapid development of SME industrial clusters. In addition, they understood that commodity trading markets may well become important sources of local fiscal income. The local government tried to improve the administration and management of the newly-built or upgraded commodity trading markets (Ke, 2012). The administrative organizations were set up within these commodity trading markets to ensure their smooth and efficient operation including the departments of finance, transport, security, telecommunications and taxation. The development of commodity trading markets, thus, became a large-scale social project dominated by the local government with the participation of professional market developers and various administrative departments (Zhu, 2003). In 2012, the provincial government of Zhejiang issued views on further promoting the development of commodity trading market, aiming to integrate market and industry, physical market and digital market further and realizing the annual trading volume of RMB2 trillion for physical and digital markets respectively (see Table 4.6).

The commodity trading market plays an important part in stimulating rural industrial development in Zhejiang Province. It acts as both distribution and phase markets by connecting local SMEs, buyers and middleman traders. The commodity trading market helps improve distribution efficiency of local SMEs through offering a transaction platform of raw materials, intermediate products, final consumer products, machinery and equipments. The high transaction volume at the market leads to the lower transaction costs with realizing scale of economy for local SMEs (Bellandi and Lombardi, 2012). Meanwhile, the commodity trading market becomes an important component of local innovation network by encouraging local SMEs to upgrade their production capability under fierce market competition (Wang, 2010).

4.4.3. *The implementation of "go out" strategy at the local level*

The central government set up a special fund to support the restructuring of the textiles industry and the efforts of Chinese textile companies to "Go Global". The Ministry of Finance, the Ministry of Commerce and the State Development and Reform Commission issued *Circular on Relevant Policies to Promote Chinese Textile Industry to Shift New Ways of Growth in Foreign Trade and Support Chinese Textile Enterprises to Go Global* in 2006, allocating a special government fund to encourage technology innovation, industrial upgrading and outward foreign direct investment by textile and clothing enterprises. In particular, the central government supports the establishment of overseas textile industrial parks by granting subsidies for loan interest, land supply, manufacturing facilities, infrastructure and supporting services. The initial scale of fund, which reached RMB800 million, was appropriated to the provincial government, which was required to formulate their own measures on the administration of the fund in accordance with the guidelines set by the central government. The amount of the fund received by each province varies proportionately with exports and overseas investment of that province.

Pursuant to the Zhejiang province's *Measures on the Administration of the Fund to Support Companies to "Go Global"* on 7 December 2005, the fund was to support the establishment of overseas commodity trading market, the manufacturing enterprises and R&D institutions, the implementation of market diversification strategy, the promotion of overseas marketing by SMEs, and the participation of overseas trade and investment fair by the enterprises (ZFTECB, 2005).

4.5. Conclusion

Both informal and formal institutions have played important roles in the SME cluster development of Zhejiang province. Among the informal institutions, social networks and rural entrepreneurial mentality are still the most important factors leading to the success of SME industrial clusters in Zhejiang province. However, the implementation of socialist market-oriented economy has gradually changed the pattern social relationships among the SMEs in the industrial clusters.

The rapid development of SME industrial clusters has also been attributed to a series of institutional innovations by the local government. The capacity and scope of intervention by the local government has varied among different development stages in Zhejiang Province. The local government has created a liberal political environment for making bottom-up institutional innovation (Zhou, 2011). In addition, it has been committed to the support for the growth of SMEs' industrial clusters and local commodity trading markets to confront the challenges of global institutional change. On the whole, the formation and development of SME industrial clusters in Zhejiang province have taken place in the interactions among informal, formal and global institutional changes.

5

THE NINGBO CLOTHING CLUSTER

5.1. Introduction

Ningbo City, which is located in the south of the Yangtze River Delta, has witnessed a history of over 7,000 years. It is a seaport and sub-provincial city located in northeastern Zhejiang Province. The city lies south of the Hangzhou Bay, borders Shaoxing City to the west, faces Sanmen Bay in the south, is adjacent to Taizhou City and is naturally sheltered by the Zhoushan Archipelago to the east. With six districts of Haishu, Jiangdong, Jiangbei, Zhenhai, Beilun and Yinzhou, three county-level cities of Yuyao, Cixi and Fenghua, and two counties of Xiangshan and Ninghai, Ningbo City covers an area of 9,817 square kilometers on land with a total population of 5.7102 million. The urban area covers 2,462 square kilometers with a population of 2.2183 million (Ningbo Municipal People's Government, 2013).

Ningbo City is an important industrial base in Zhejiang Province. It has formed an industrial structure mainly composed of traditional industries, such as textiles, garments, machinery, large-scale harbor-based industries represented by petrochemicals, iron and steel, power generation, paper-making, and hi-tech industry including the integration of electronic information, mechanical and electrical engineering, biomedicine and so on. In 2011, the GDP of the city reached RMB601.5 billion. The GDP per capita reached RMB76,941 (USD12,213). The budgetary revenue income hit RMB143.18 billion, including the local revenue of RMB65.76 billion. The city ranks the ninth among all the sub-provincial cities of China by its GDP, the fourth by local revenue income and the third by disposable income of urban residents (Ningbo Municipal Statistics Bureau, 2012).

Ningbo City is one of the three major clothing production bases in China. Its output accounts for about one-twelfth of the national total. Ningbo is also one of the important production bases of men's wear in the world. Its clothing products have been exported to over 80 countries and regions. Many famous brands such as Firs, Youngor, Romon, Progen, Rouse, Peacebird, and Veken have been created and developed. Most of the clothing firms have agglomerated in an area of 15 kilometers between Duantan Town, Yinzhou District and Jiangkou Town, Fenghua City. The clothing firms in Ningbo City mainly produce shirts and suits, children's wear, knitted dresses, leather wear, silk clothes and so on. The output, sales and the number of famous brands are all at the top of the league tables in China.

5.2. The Formation and Development of Ningbo Clothing Cluster

The clothing industry in Ningbo City has witnessed a long history. Ningbo was the port of departure of "the silk road in the sea" in ancient China. The tailors from Cixi County, Ningbo City, known as *"Zhe Ci Bang"*, were famous for making traditional Chinese clothes and monopolized the clothing industry in Beijing between the 1680s and 1930s. However, those from Yinzhou district and Fenghua City, the *"Hongbang"* tailors, did not enter Shanghai City until the end of the 18th century. They grasped the skills of making western-style suits after communicating with foreigners living in the foreign concessions of Shanghai. The two schools of tailors, who used to make Western-style suits outside Ningbo City, imparted their skills around Ningbo City through their social networks. Therefore, Ningbo City has enjoyed its special position in the historic development of the clothing industry in China. For example, the tailors in Ningbo City made the first tunic suit and Western-style suit, managed the first Western-style suit store and founded the first clothing-making school in China (Qian, 1999).

After the founding of the People's Republic of China in 1949, the cooperatives initially created by villages and towns were turned into clothing factories in the 1950s, which made military uniforms and embroidered dresses in the 1960s and uniforms in the 1970s. The TVEs developed very fast after China adopted the open-door policy in 1978. The output rose by 30% annually before 1983. Ningbo City became one of the processing bases for clothing companies headquartered in Shanghai. Afterwards, a number of Shanghai-affiliated clothing factories emerged. Some industrial clothing companies were established to manage the large collective clothing enterprises in the mid-1980s.

The transformation of enterprise system in Ningbo took place after Deng Xiaoping's southern tour speech in 1992. For instance, Shanshan Group achieved great success in establishing its own brand and many other local clothing firms followed suit. Subsequently, Shanshan Group and Youngor Group were listed on the Shanghai Stock Exchange in 1996 and 1998 respectively. The private clothing firms mushroomed in the region after 1999 when the status of the private sector was officially recognized in the Chinese Constitution. A wave of establishing joint-venture clothing firms has emerged since 2000. Ningbo City has become one of OEM production centers in China, emphasizing design with high flexible specialization and a relatively complete industrial chain (Table 5.1).

5.3. Informal Institutions and Cluster Development

The certain "Ningbo Merchants" debuted in the Ming Dynasty, developed in Shanghai after the Opium War in the 1840s, and reached their heyday after the democratic revolution in 1911. Ningbo Merchants played an important role in the development of modern industry and commerce in China. At the end of Qing Dynasty, Ningbo businesspeople created several records in Shanghai, including the first bank, the first private shipping company, the first modern wool plant, the first silent short film of China, and the first Red Cross organization in China. At the moment, there are still 300,000 "Ningbo Merchants" and their descendants living in some 60 overseas countries and regions, who have helped to forge the international linkages of Ningbo clothing cluster (Ningbo Municipal People's Government, 2013).

Social networks have played an important role in the development of Ningbo clothing cluster. With the advantage of wide social networks in Shanghai, the entrepreneurs in Ningbo had access to the purchase of fabrics and other raw materials and gained the clothing-making skills in the

Table 5.1. The development of Ningbo clothing cluster.

Development stages	Market demand	The features of garment industrial cluster	Representative enterprises
The initial stage (1949 to 1978)	The making of ready-to-wear clothes started with limited market demand.	— The cooperatives initially created by villages and towns were turned into clothing factories. — The initial stage mainly dealt with the processing of supplied material. Military uniforms and embroidered dresses were made in the 1960s and suits in the mid- to late-1970s. — The clothes-making equipments were simple and the industrial development was slow. — Industrial scale was low: There were 76 garments factories with 4,780 employees in 1980.	Ningbo Embroidery Dress Factory and Ningbo Clothing Factory.

(Continued)

Table 5.1. (*Continued*)

Development stages	Market demand		The features of garment industrial cluster	Representative enterprises
The growth stage (From the end of 1970s to the mid-1980s)	The economic development and increasing foreign exchanges led to changes in fashion and promoted the rapid development of the ready-made clothes industry; the garment market was not mature; the mid-1980s witnessed the start of the fashion for wearing western suits throughout China.	—	Ningbo became the processing base for Shanghai and for overseas companies depending on its location advantage and good social relations.	Yinzhou District Textile and Garments Factory, Fenghua Roman Suits Factory, Yinzhou District Pei Luo Chen Suits Factory, Ningbo Suits Factory affiliated with Shanghai Kai Kai Company
		—	The clothes factories were set up throughout Ningbo, most of which were in Fenghua City.	
		—	Suits were mainly made in Jiangkou Town, Fenghua City and Yinzhou District; shirts in Chunhu District.	
		—	Initially processing for the clothes factories in Shanghai and some Shanghai affiliated factories emerged later.	
		—	Technology and operation were updated, but capital accumulation was slow.	
		—	The clothes market was immature and unstable, resulting in the rapid creation and bankruptcy of small enterprises.	
		—	The industry reached a greater scale with 825 clothes enterprises and 6,370 employees. The output hit 35.51 million units.	

(*Continued*)

Table 5.1. (*Continued*)

Development stages	Market demand	The features of garment industrial cluster	Representative enterprises
The transition stage (The mid- and late-1980s)	Suits were out of fashion.	— A large number of lagged enterprises went bankrupt. — The medium-sized enterprises introduced some new equipment and improved the grade and quality of their products. — Some garment industrial companies were established, managing the state-owned, large collective clothes enterprises and TVEs (Township and Village enterprises). — Some enterprises created their own brands and some products were given awards by ministry and provincial government, but the market value of brands and awards was not recognized.	Yingzhou District Qing Chun Garment Factory, Ningbo Yong Gang Garment Factory, and Roman Suits Factory.

(Continued)

Table 5.1. (*Continued*)

Development stages	Market demand	The features of garment industrial cluster	Representative enterprises
The development stage (In the 1990s)	The clothes market has been relatively saturated; the demand for the middle- and high-grade clothes is high; new cultural elements have been reflected in the clothing industry; the consumption psychology is increasingly mature and the value of famous brands has been strengthened.	— Shanshan Enterprise achieved great success in establishing its own brand, promoting the emergence of branded enterprises. — Some leading enterprises are moving towards the establishment of world famous brands. — The brand helps to differentiate the local garment enterprises. It also spaces out the differences in garment enterprises between Ningbo City and other areas, establishing the regional brand — Ningbo Clothes. — A fever for establishing joint-venture garment enterprises has emerged. — The government has attached more importance to the garment industry and improved the development environment of the garment industry. — The professional garment organizations (institutes, testing centers) and the garment associations have been established and the production system has been basically completed.	Youngor Group, Shan Shan Group, Roman Group, Rouse Group, and Progen Group.

(*Continued*)

Table 5.1.   *(Continued)*

Development stages	Market demand	The features of garment industrial cluster	Representative enterprises
The upgrading and internationalization stage since 2000	The domestic and overseas demand for the middle- and high-quality clothes is high.	— Ningbo City has become one of OEM production centers in China. — Some clothing firms have made outward foreign direct investment. — The brands of some clothing's firms have been gradually internationalized.	Youngor Group and Shan Shan Group.

Sources: Qian (1999) and the fieldwork by the author.

planned economic era, which made it possible for Ningbo City to become one of the important processing bases for Shanghai. A lot of people in Ningbo City, who used to make clothes for foreigners, were well known as *"Hong Bang Sewingmen"*. They were active players in the fashion circles of Shanghai City. After the liberation in 1949, some Ningbo-ese went to Shanghai City to learn modern clothing-making skills and then returned to set up their own clothing firms, thanks to the sibling, kinship and regional ties. In addition, some experts in Shanghai City were invited to Ningbo City to provide professional guidance and help to establish business relationships. A lot of SMEs in the Ningbo clothing cluster were developed rapidly by taking advantage of the unique social networks there (Zhu, 2003).

Ningbo Progen Group Co., Ltd. is one of the typical examples. Jiangliu village is located in the neighborhood of Ningbo City and there are about 502 households. In 1984, Liying Shi and 19 female villagers set up Jiangliu Village Synthetic Fiber and Labor Protection Products Factory with RMB1,000. The factory mainly produced gloves, aprons, oversleeves and so on. In 1985, she learned from *Ningbo Daily* that Chengfa Lu, Super Master of western style suits in Shanghai City, gave guidance on the establishment of western-style suits factory in Ningbo City and worked as a technical consultant there. He had developed new sewing templates of western-style suits particularly for the Asian people and pioneered the industry. Liying Shi was also surprised to learn that Chengfa Lu was born in Jiangliu village, and then she had the idea of employing the Super Master for the township enterprise. Master Lu was moved by her sincerity and agreed to help his villagers to run a clothing business. He helped Liying Shi to set up a joint venture (Progen Western Style Suits Factory) with Shanghai Textile Bureau. In the beginning, Master Lu worked as a technical consultant for the factory and was mainly responsible for training the sewingmen. In the following two years, Liying Shi found that western-style suits became more and more popular all over China and she was determined to develop the essence of *"Hong Bang Sewingmen"*. One comfortable western style suit was the incarnation of diligence, hardship and innovation of *"Hong Bang Sewingmen"*. In 1987, Master Lu was invited to take up the post of technical director at Progen Western Style Suits Factory, which was renamed Ningbo Progen Clothng Company in

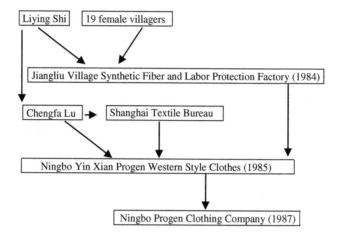

Fig. 5.1.   Social network and the establishment of Ningbo Progen Group Co., Ltd.
Source: Compiled by the author.

the same year (Fig. 5.1). There are about 300 sewingmen in the company who have received the instruction of Master Lu. The tradition of *"Hong Bang Sewingmen"* has been inherited and disseminated in the industrial cluster. Therefore, the social network has contributed greatly to the rapid growth of SMEs in the clothing cluster (Ying *et al.*, 2007).

5.4. Formal Institutions and Cluster Development

In the course of development of Ningbo clothing cluster, the role of Ningbo Municipal Government has continued to change. The regional development in Ningbo City conformed to the "Sunan model" in the 1980s. That is, collectively-owned TVEs dominated the economy and Ningbo Municipal Government interfered with the management of enterprises through government appointed agents. In the 1990s, however, as collective enterprises exposed their shortcomings to include rigid mechanisms, inefficient operations and fuzzy property rights, Ningbo Municipal Government took a series of measures to undertake shareholding restructuring and encourage the development of the private economy.

The restructuring and privatization of the SOEs took place in the late 1990s and at the beginning of 2000s. At the end of 1997, the central government of China deepened the reform of SOEs and aimed to invigorate them within three years. Ningbo Municipal Government reorganized 42 state-owned textile companies and established Ningbo VEKEN Group Shareholding Co., Ltd. in May 1998. However, due to the lack of ownership reform, the newly-found VEKEN Group inevitably confronted various systematic defects. For example, 11,033 out of 18,678 employees were retired. It was highly important for the local government to initiate a new round of more fundamental reform to establish a modern enterprise system with a corporate legal personnel management system. In 2000, Ningbo Municipal Government issued *Several Opinions on Straightening out Labor Relations of Municipal Enterprises and Opinions on Deepening the Reform of State-Owned Enterprises*. Afterwards, the reform of property rights and labor relations were carried out in the form of Management Buyout (MBO). The ownership reform was completed successfully under the guidance of local government. In 2004, the total assets of the group reached RMB4.2 billion with the profits of RMB300 million (NBEC, 2005). The restructured SOEs have contributed to the rapid development of local clothing cluster.

In the process of ownership transformation, Ningbo Municipal Government has devoted itself more to the public services including the improvement of local infrastructure, the simplification of project application procedures and the movement towards the e-government so as to create a sound business environment. It has shown that a developmental state plays a proactive role in formulating an explicit development blueprint to stimulate the local industrial development and internationalize the region. Ningbo Municipal Government has been actively involved in industrial planning to change the previously weak cohesion and excessive competition of clustered firms to make full use of regional resources and improve the competitiveness of the clothing cluster. It has constructed industrial parks where clothing firms agglomerate to improve collective efficiency. It has played an important role in creating a sound industrial investment environment. Moreover, Ningbo Entry-Exit Inspection and Quarantine Bureau established Ningbo Textile Products Testing Centre in 1984 to help the clothing firms in the cluster to test the quality of fabrics and other textile products (Wang *et al.*, 2007).

In order to help the local clothing firms to develop international markets and improve the international images of their brands, Ningbo

Municipal Government has held the Ningbo International Fashion Festival annually since 1997, which has helped to improve the international image of Ningbo clothing cluster. The China International Fashion Trading Fair is one of the top five fashion fairs in China. The 15th fair in 2011 attracted more than 600 clothing firms, 100 international fashion brands and over 5,000 overseas buyers.

5.5. The Internationalization of Ningbo Clothing Cluster

Ningbo Municipal Government supports the clothing firms in the cluster to diversify and internationalize business to improve their competitive advantage. In the past three decades, some SMEs in Ningbo clothing cluster have gradually developed into large-scale business groups centered on a holding company with diversified business to include finance, real estate and public health, all previously monopolized by the public sector (Wang *et al.*, 2007). The Youngor Group is a typical and significant example of this process. It has been seeking to become one of the largest clothing firms in the world. The company has been sticking to its own brand strategy while developing high value-added products to meet the increasing demands of the domestic market. While maintaining its market share of men's suits, it has also entered into leisurewear, endeavoring to expand its international market and exporting clothes with its own brand instead of conducting OEM for overseas clients. The entrepreneurs of Youngor Group have successfully implemented a vertical integration strategy and a diversification strategy, making the group one of the most competitive clothing firms in China. In addition, the entrepreneurs in the group have been trying to make the group go global by forming strategic alliances with the leading textile and fashion firms in the world. The evolution of the vertical integration strategy at Youngor Group consists of the following stages (Table 5.2).

Individual workshop processing. Youth Garment Factory, the predecessor of Youngor Group, was established in 1979 with about 20 young employees. In 1983, it started to undertake the processing for Shanghai Kai Kai Shirts Company, which provided the trademark, technology and information. The projects of Youth Garment Factory increased considerably by forming alliance with the leading state-owned shirt-marking company in China (Youngor Group, 2013).

Table 5.2. The evolution of vertical integration strategy and marketing network of Youngor Group.

History	Textiles	Clothes	Marketing network
Past (1979)	Processing with supplied material or purchase from other domestic firms.	Individual workshop processing — OEM of domestic shirts.	The marketing channels of domestic state-owned clothing firms.
	Purchasing from other domestic firms.	Expanding the scale of production.	Domestic wholesaling and retailing markets.
	Processing with supplied material or purchasing from other domestic and international firms.	Expanding the scale of production, OEM of international brand.	The marketing channels of international firms.
	Purchase from other domestic and international firms.	Producing and marketing its own brand.	Organizing the distribution channels (regions/branches/self-supporting/shopping centers/franchise and so on).
Present	Establishing joint ventures with other domestic and international firms producing fabrics.	Producing at the newly-built firms in western regions.	The primary integration of domestic marketing channels.
	Relocating of fabric producing workshops.	Establishing Youngor as one of leading international brands.	The integration of domestic and international marketing channels; multi-brand operation.

Source: Xiao *et al.* (2006) and the author's interviews.

Traditional wholesale business. With the deepening economic reform in the middle of 1980s, Youngor Group grasped several good opportunities and expanded its scale of business. It created its own brand "Beilun Port" and the sales of shirts had hit 3 million units by the end of 1986 (Youngor Group, 2013). The penetration into the retailing market changed the market structure of the enterprise. Although the management system was not changed, the enterprise became aware of the concept of the market economy. The subsequent corporate strategy was formulated to satisfy the market demand. Meanwhile, the processing charges, the added value of the raw materials and the profits of the wholesale business led to initial capital accumulation for the expansion of the firm (Xiao *et al.*, 2006).

International OEM. At the beginning of the 1990s, the demand for garment processing from international firms with well-known brands promoted the rapid development of the clothing industry in China. Its overall progress was also stimulated by the development of the domestic clothing market. Youngor Group was one of the representative enterprises that grew up at this stage. Youth Garment Factory established one joint venture called Youngor Clothing Company Limited with Namkqong Trading Company Limited in Macao in 1990, officially launching the "Youngor" brand (Youngor Group, 2013). The capacity to make clothes was mainly driven by the high-demand for ready-made clothes. The constant introduction of advanced manufacturing techniques and efficient management methods at the previous stages made it possible to realize economies of scale, improve product quality and reduce production costs along the learning curve. It laid a solid foundation for establishing a good reputation for Youngor brand in China. The successful implementation of its brand strategy accelerated the rapid expansion of the enterprise.

Producing and marketing in its own brands. In the 1980s, more than 4,000 state-owned department stores formed partnerships with Youngor Group, but a lot of them closed down or went bankrupt as competition became fiercer at the beginning of the 1990s (Xiao *et al.*, 2006). As the number of business partners fell, the senior managers of Youngor Group promoted their brand image more aggressively. In 1995, Youngor Group set up Youngor Clothing Company Limited as a modern marketing company, which was mainly engaged in the establishment of a marketing network for cultivating its own brand, expanding the target market and improving corporate profits. Currently, it operates a network of over 100 branch offices and over 400 company-owned stores, and over 2,000 outlets across China, forming a diversified marketing network (Youngor Group, 2013). Youngor Group has achieved great success in the primary market of branded ready-made clothes. The market structure of Youngor Group changed with the upgrading of the clothing industry in China. The enterprise has been transformed from a clothing-making factory mainly engaged in the wholesale and OEM business into a diversified enterprise group specializing in the making and marketing of clothes with its own brands. The huge profits resulting from its strong brand image led to the accumulation of more capital and talents for the further development of the enterprise (Xiao *et al.*, 2006).

Vertical integration strategy. To realize the strategy of vertical integration, a "Textile Town" was constructed in 2002 by Youngor Group with several leading Japanese *keiretsu*, with Youngor Group accounting for 70% of the ownership and the *keiretsu* 30%, engaging in a range of processes from cotton spinning to printing, dyeing and finishing, wool spinning and synthetic fiber programs (Wang *et al.*, 2007). More and more international giants such as Next and Gap have linked with Youngor Group to procure high-quality fabrics. Meanwhile, with the rapid development of the clothing industry in China generally, the domestic demand for high-quality fabrics continues to rise fast. There is still ample room for developing high-quality fabrics in the near future and the group intends to take advantage of vertical integration strategy to improve its competitiveness (Youngor Group, 2013).

Youngor Group can compete against most leading firms in the making of ready-to-wear clothes because it has been involved in OEM for many leading international brands including some strict Japanese customers for many years. However, there is still a wide gap between the quality of the fabrics produced at home and those produced abroad since most of the fabrics are still made with traditional means and the inputs are still limited in the Ningbo clothing cluster generally. Youngor Group has reduced its domestic purchases because of the demand for high-quality fabrics. In order to meet the challenges imposed by China's accession to the WTO, Youngor Group has been trying to expand its international sales in recent years. It established a subsidiary in Japan. In addition, it set up partnerships with the leading Japanese textile and clothing companies such as Itochu and Marubeni. But Japanese firms are concerned that Youngor Group may not maintain the high quality of its fabrics in terms of color, strength, density and environmental standards.

Another reason for the adoption of vertical integration strategy is the high price of imported fabric as a result of high import tariffs levied. The lagging behind of the printing, dyeing and finishing of textile products has constrained the further development of the clothing industry in China (Zhang, 2009). The current brands under Youngor Group include MAYOR, YOUNGOR, GY, HAMP, FAMILY, and Hart Schaffner Marx. MAYOR, CEO, and GY are the Youngor Group's own brands targeting civil servants, businessmen, young and trendy groups respectively while Hemp Family is one self-developed new brand for green hemp products (Youngor Group, 2013). Youngor Group signed agreements with Japanese *keiretsu* Itochu and the Italian company Marzotto in Ningbo at the end of 2005, forming one of the biggest global textile and clothing alliances in terms of technology, capital, training and marketing with the primary aim of evading world trade barriers and expanding the high-end textile and clothing market. At the beginning of 2003, Youngor Group invested USD40 million alongside Itochu to set up one joint venture specializing in refined wool textiles. It has gained a competitive advantage in the international market by introducing globally advanced equipments for dyeing, weaving and finishing (Liu, 2006).

Itochu, the biggest sales dealer of fiber products around the globe, is one of the most important business partners of Youngor Group. With the help of Itochu, the subsidiary of the Youngor group in Tokyo has expanded its business so rapidly that it is regarded as one of the companies with most growth potential in the 21st century by the Japanese media. Meanwhile, the Italian Company Marzotto, has a 200 year-old history owning a series of the world's leading brands including Hugo Boss and Valentino. At present, it is also one of the biggest suppliers of textile fabrics in Europe. In order to meet the global competition of textile and clothing industry, Marzotto had the intention of expanding its investment in China, looking for its new strategic partner in Asia. Originally it planned to become a majority shareholder in a Chinese textile company or set up a new high-quality textile company. In the end, it decided to form strategic alliances with Youngor Group and Itochu Keiretsu to expand its global share. As explained above, there is a substantial gap in the production of high-quality textile fabrics between China and western countries (Liu, 2006). In recent years, Youngor group has established some joint trading institutions in the United States,

Japan and Hong Kong, trying to establish its own overseas marketing channels. The cooperation with Itochu and Marzotto has been one of the most important strategies adopted by Youngor Group in its expansion into the high-end market and its arrival as an important player on the international clothing market.

The joint venture between Youngor Group, Itochu and Marzotto, has provided exclusive production skills and technology boosted by new investment, technology transfer and marketing channels, improving the competitiveness of all three corporations. Italian manufacturing equipment has arrived at the Youngor Industrial Park in Ningbo and Italian experts visit Youngor Group regularly to supervise the production. Italy is well known for its textile and clothing industry with a lot of international brands. It also has a mature flow of production, technology, workshop management, advanced marketing models, global networks and complete marketing systems. The Chinese textile and clothing companies have lower labor cost and diligent workers. Japan has advanced management models and rich experience of international operations. The strategic alliance formed by these three leading enterprises in the world allows it to take advantage of their respective competitive edges and strengthen the competitive advantage of each (Liu, 2006).

Competition among modern enterprises lies in time, cost and quality of the whole supply chain. The construction of "Textile Town" by Youngor Group has not only reduced transport and transaction costs with fabrics suppliers, but also ensured that the quality of fabrics for ready-to-wear clothes keeps up with international fashions. Youngor Group expects to reach the international level of making fabrics and strengthen its core competitive advantage. The advantages of Youngor Group's vertical integration strategy are as follows: (a) Economies of Scale. The high demand for ready-to-wear clothes and marketing network can ensure the realization of economies of scale. The moving towards the upper stream will save a large amount of transportation costs and transaction costs, reducing the cost of ready-to-wear clothes in the end. (b) Reorganizing the operation. The enterprise will be able to benefit more from the operation and reorganization since most of partners are the leading international textile firms. Moving towards the upper stream is based on the quick response of whole supply chain. The non-core business activities will be subcontracted to external specialized firms. The development and production of fabrics have become the core activities of Youngor Group. The introduction of advanced technology and scientific management will fill in the gap of producing, printing and dyeing, after finishing of domestic advanced fabrics. (c) Risk sharing. The utilization of external resources will reduce the risks of investment and improve the adjustment capacity to the changes of business environment. The R&D and management of Youngor Group will be geared to international standards through establishing the joint venture of "Textile Town" (Xiao *et al.*, 2006).

Diversification strategy. Youngor Group started to enter into the development of high-quality residential apartments and the provision of supporting services with the advantages of large land reserves and capital in 1992 (Wang *et al.*, 2007). The gross profits of this real estate development business rose steadily before 2009, but declined in 2010 and 2011 due to the strict regulation of property market by the central government of China (Table 5.3). The gross profits of Youngor Real Estate Development Corporation reached RMB1.19 billion in 2009 (The Youngor Group, 2010). Youngor Group maintains its leading position in the real estate sector in Ningbo City.

The board of directors of Youngor Group Joint Stock Co., Ltd. decided to invest RMB320 million to become a founding member of CITIC Securities Co., Ltd. on 5 August 2001 (The Youngor Group, 2003). Youngor Group made the investment as a means of tapping the capital market while adhering to its clothing business. In 2006, Youngor Group made huge profits as a shareholder of CITIC Securities Co., Ltd. with the prosperous capital market in China (The Youngor Group, 2007). However, its earnings from the capital market have declined since the outbreak of global financial crisis in 2007.

Table 5.3. The gross profits of Youngor Group in clothing and real estate development between 2007 and 2011 (RMB100 million).

	2007	2008	2009	2010	2011
Clothing	-	4.89	4.45	7.04	6.91
Real estate	-	7.78	11.9	6.79	5.71

Sources: The Youngor Group (2008, 2009, 2010, 2011, 2012).

More and more clustered firms including Shanshan Group, Peacebird Group, Louse Group and Progen Group in Ningbo clothing cluster have also adopted the diversification strategy as they make further business expansion. However, none of the clothing firms intends to leave the clothing industry (Wang *et al.*, 2007).

Internationalization strategy. In 2008, Youngor Group acquired XinMa Apparel International Limited with USD120 million. Under the acquisition, Youngor Group received 14 manufacturing bases of XinMa in Sri Lanka, the Philippines and the Chinese mainland. XinMa, affiliated to Kellwood Company of the United States, is one of the three biggest apparel companies in Hong Kong. It has developed a wide network of distributors, clients, logistics and distribution worldwide (Xinhua News, 2008). With international acquisition, Youngor Group has realized the integration of clothing industrial chain and formed a complete operation system from the upstream to the retailing sector. In addition, it has grasped some core technology to upgrade the clothing products. The shirts business has witnessed 30% growth since the cooperation (Liu, 2012).

In addition to Youngor Group, other clothing firms in the cluster are also in the course of internationalization. For example, Shenzhou International Group Holdings Limited, Mingda Knitting Group Co., Ltd. and Hongmei Textile & Garments Co., Ltd. are three typical firms in Ningbo clothing cluster that have made outward foreign direct investment successfully in the less developed countries in the Asia-Pacific region (Wang *et al.*, 2009).

Shenzhou (Cambodia) Company Limited (Shenzhou Cambodia) is a wholly owned subsidiary created by Shenzhou International Group Holdings Limited with an investment of USD3.8 million in June 2005. It specializes in the manufacture and sale of knitwear products at two rented factory buildings covering 15,500 square meters and the newly-built auxiliary buildings with 5,000 square meters in Vattanac industrial park, Phnom Penh. Shenzhou Cambodia started production in September 2005 and realized profits in June 2006. It mainly serves North American customers and has gone through the factory inspections successfully by the world famous clients including NIKE, ADIDAS, PUMA and UNIQLO. In June 2006, the board of directors decided to increase its investment by

USD300 million. Cambodia has become the major and established manufacturing base of the Group with the constant expansion of production capacity so as to ensure the stable and timely supply of products to customers and achieve the stable profitability in accordance with the overall strategic arrangement of Group.

Shenzhou International Group Holdings Limited is the largest integrated knitwear manufacturer in China. The company mainly specializes in manufacturing high-quality knitwear on an Original Equipment Manufacture basis. Covering 900,000 square meters at Ningbo Economic and Technical Development Zone, the annual output of knitwear exceeds 110 million pieces in 2013. The product line of the company ranges from casual wear to sportswear for the major international renowned sportswear brands including NIKE, ADIDAS, PUMA and UNIQLO. The company also possesses the capacity of knitting, printing, embroidery, dyeing and finishing. Its export destination has extended from Japan to Europe, the United States and the whole Asia-Pacific region. In November 2005, Shenzhou International was listed on the Main Board of Hong Kong Stock Exchange (Shenzhou International Group Holdings Limited, 2013).

Ningbo New Mingda (Cambodia) Manufacture Co., Ltd. was established in Vattanac Industrial Park, Phnom Penh with an investment of about USD3 million in 2006. The company is a subsidiary of Ningbo Mingda Knitting Group Co., Ltd. (Mingda Group), controlled by Ningbo Shanshan Co., Ltd., one of the leading textile and clothing enterprise in Ningbo clothing cluster. All the knitting products made by Mingda Group target the international market. The sound regional industrial environment and the scale effects by local textile and clothing clusters partly trade off the negative effects of trade frictions and RMB appreciation. Mingda Group started to produce the knitting products in 1974. Currently, it ranks Top Three in the knitting sector of Ningbo textile and clothing cluster. It has a relatively complete production line, owning one trading company and 12 factories in weaving, dyeing, embroidering, cutting out and sewing (Mingda Group, 2013).

Ningbo Hongmei (Cambodia) Textile and Clothing Co., Ltd. was established in Canadia Industrial Park, Phnom Penh by Ningbo Hongmei Textile & Garments Co., Ltd. with an investment of USD1 million in March 2006. It has a capacity of making 1 million shirts every year.

Ningbo Hongmei Textile & Garments Co., Ltd. is a joint venture with Chile established in March 2003. It is an integrated export-oriented enterprise with a total investment of USD2.1 million. The company is mainly engaged in R&D, design, production, marketing and service of garments. The main products include jackets, men's, women's, children's shirts, casual and beach pants. Its products are exported to Europe, the United States, Canada, the South America, Australia, New Zealand, South Korea and Hong Kong (Hongmei Garmnet Company, 2013).

The above three textile and clothing firms have created a set of effective management methods to develop successful subsidiaries in Cambodia and contributed to the inclusive development of the least developed countries in the Asia-Pacific region.

Shenzhou International Group Holdings Limited is one typical successful example. First, it has adopted an intensive management model and introduced its corporate culture to Cambodia successfully. The company sent about 70 Chinese managerial and technical staff to teach Cambodian workers by personal example and verbal instruction in the beginning so that Cambodian workers could form good working habits, improve their skills gradually and strengthen their awareness of quality. The company entered into the right path quickly. Within three years, the number of garment workers increased to 5,000 and the monthly output rose from 150,000 to 1.3 million pieces. The company has met the global manufacturer's standards set by international famous brands such as NIKE and Adidas and passed their factory inspections successfully.

Second, Shenzhou Cambodia strengthens its communication with the local workers. The workers' representatives and trade union can become the driving force of corporate growth if the enterprise cooperates with them well. In addition, the enterprise has set up a suggestion box at each workshop. The garment workers can put forward their suggestions and viewpoints to the managers. If their problems cannot be solved satisfactorily in the context of Cambodian law and regulations, the managers will make explanations to the employees involved. All of the potential problems need to be nipped in the bud so that garment workers are able to work happily. The Chinese managers have also grasped the local language and communicate with the local workers effectively.

Third, the good working environment has contributed to the improve-ment of Cambodian workers' efficiency. The local workers' efficiency was only 50% of those in China at the beginning, but it increased by 20% after adopting the piecework wage.

Fourth, the production capacity and ancillary facilities of Shenzhou Cambodia have expanded progressively, which have contributed to the formation of complete garment value chain in Cambodia. For example, Shenzhou Cambodia set up a printing and embroidery production line in 2007 to better satisfy the needs of customers. Shenzhou Cambodia has become a stable production base in the Southeast Asian region for the company.

The clients of Ningbo Hongmei Textile & Garments Co., Ltd. are mainly in South America, so the company does not face high trade barriers for their exports. However, the fiercer domestic competition and apprecia-tion of RMB have forced the company to relocate some of the production in Cambodia. The profit margin of exports from Cambodia can be 2–3% higher than those from the mainland, particularly to the US and EU market.

The Ningbo clothing cluster has accelerated its pace of internation-alization since late 1990s. For example, the subsidiaries in Cambodia have been gradually integrating into the vertically-integrated value chain of textile and clothing firms in China, thereby becoming an important node in global textile and clothing value chain and realizing the successful inclusive development. LDCs can be part of regional production network of China. The inclusive development can be further promoted when the textile and clothing industry in the Asia-Pacific LDCs such as Cambodia and Bangladesh are integrated into global value chain through forging industrial linkage with China. Some firms in Ningbo clothing cluster have firm-specific advantages over those in the LDCs of Asia-Pacific region. The means of south–south cooperation can range from outsourcing to technology transfer, the dissemination of advanced management model and the implementation of cluster policy. More and more Chinese textile and clothing enterprises that have made investment in Cambodia have relatively complete value chain. They have the capability to establish more complete value chain within SEZs in Cambodia (Wang *et al.*, 2009).

5.6. Conclusion

The Ningbo clothing cluster was formed and developed on the basis of its geographic, economic and social conditions. Informal, formal and global institutions have been closely related to the growth and upgrading of cluster. In the initial period of development, some community members with entrepreneurship and market consciousness took advantage of their social networks, gained advanced clothing-making skills and grasped market opportunities from their fellow villagers in Shanghai City. With the support of the local government, they established collective clothing firms. The achievements of entrepreneurs encouraged the local people to set up more clothing firms, which led to the formation of clothing cluster in the 1990s. The capital accumulation and technological achievements of TVEs and SOEs in the 1980s and early 1990s laid a solid foundation for the formation of Ningbo clothing cluster and the growth of SMEs in the cluster. Meanwhile, the entrepreneurs accelerated institutional innovation and technological innovation with the help of the local government. The implementation of brand strategy has improved the competitiveness of industrial cluster.

The LDCs in the Asia-Pacific region can be integrated into the value chain of some leading firms in Ningbo clothing cluster because they have great demand for raw materials and textile machinery produced in China. However, China maintains trade surplus with all LDCs. The exports from the Asia-Pacific LDCs to China are very limited (Yan, 2008). The OFDI of Chinese textile and clothing firms have also promoted the exports of yarn, fabrics, textile machinery and equipment to the Asia-Pacific LDCs.

The governments in China and the Asia-Pacific LDCs need to cultivate the vertical market linkages in the textile and clothing sector through implementing more powerful industrial promotion schemes because the textile and garment exports of LDCs usually rely on a few foreign companies. Some of the large-scale textile and clothing firms in China are already making efforts to set up the supporting industries in the LDCs. For example, Shenzhou International has already established an embroidery workshop in Cambodia in 2007. The enterprises' voluntary behavior needs to be guided and supported by the host country's industrial policy and blueprints. The Asia-Pacific LDCs should have more incentives and support for developing backwards linkage of local enterprises to deepen the supply chain. Meanwhile, the LDCs Cambodian government should try to increase its textile production with the reduction of raw material costs so that the textile industry and the garment sector can be more competitive.

6

SHAOXING TEXTILE CLUSTER

6.1. Introduction

Shaoxing City, situated in the southern corner of the Yangtze River delta and the mid-northern part of Zhejiang Province, covers an area of 8,256 square kilometers with a population of about 4.4 million. It has six administrative divisions including Yuecheng District, Shaoxing County, Shangyu City, Shengzhou City, Xinchang County and Zhuji City with 118 township-level subdistricts and townships. It is one of the largest textile cities in China with over 2,500 textile and clothing enterprises. It is also the important production base of synthetic fibers in Zhejiang province (Shaoxing Municipal Government, 2013). Shaoxing City has formed a complete textile industrial chain, ranging from synthetic fiber raw materials, textile products, printing and dyeing, garments and textile machinery (see Table 6.1). Since 1988, the Shaoxing textile cluster has witnessed a rapid increase of textile exports. In 2012, the textile and clothing exports of Shaoxing City reached USD17.197 billion (Shaoxing City States).

Shaoxing textile cluster is made up of some sub-clusters located in different districts and counties. The urban area of Shaoxing county is mainly engaged in fabrics and synthetic fiber; Shangyu City in cotton textiles; Shenzhou City in ties; and Xinchan County in wool spinning and knitting machinery. Some leading firms have emerged in each sub-cluster. For example, the output of Zhejiang Long Shen Group Shareholding Co., Ltd. accounts for about 21% of world dyestuff market. Zhejiang Yong Tong Dyeing and Knitting Group Co., Ltd. is one of the Top 10 dyeing and printing enterprises in China; Busen group Co., Ltd. is one of the leading clothing firms in China.

Table 6.1. The production capacity of Shaoxing textile cluster in 2012.

Products	Production capacity
Polyester (PET)	1.4843 million tons
Polyester fiber	4.3566 million meters
Fabrics	5.194 billion meters
Dyed Fabrics	20.147 billion meters
Clothes	373 million units
Ties	147.77 million units
Printing and dyeing raw material	705, 344 tons
Socks	4,675.21 million pairs

Sources: The Shaoxing City Statistics Bureau (2013) and the author's fieldwork.

China Textile City, located in Shaoxing County, has become the largest distribution center of textile products in Asia with a turnover of RMB55.704 billion in 2012. It hosts Qianqing Light Textile Raw Material Market and Fabric Market at Dongsheng Road. About 19 textile trading markets are distributed in the four transaction areas, covering an area of 523,000 square meters (China Textile City, 2013). The textile commodity trading market has contributed to the formation and development of SME textile clusters in Shaoxing City, leading to the rapid industrial development in the region.

6.2. The Informal Institutional Change and the Development of Shaoxing Textile Cluster

Informal institutions play an important role in the formation and development of Shaoxing textile cluster. Shaoxing City has a long textile history. The rural farmers, who have been engaged in sericulture cultivation and textile industry, have accumulated rich experiences and skills of making textile products. It has become one of important sources of competitive advantages of Shaoxing textile cluster. At the beginning of Qing Dynasty, a large number of Shaoxingnese left for Shanghai City. Because they were earnest and down-to-earth, some of them became business tycoons. With the mercantilism spirits deeply embedded in the local culture, the people in Shaoxing City have developed the human spirits of utilitarianism, firm commitment, hard work and strategic planning with wisdom, which have great impacts on the formation and growth of Shaoxing textile cluster (Zhu *et al.*, 2008).

Social network is crucial to the new venture creation and the development of inter-firm cooperation in Shaoxing textile cluster. When rural entrepreneurs started to establish new businesses at the beginning of 1980s, the SOEs possessed the majority of social resources. In order to overcome the shortage of capital and technology, entrepreneurs in rural Shaoxing had to make use of social network to seek resources and discover opportunities. Meanwhile, social network is also an important channel to disseminate new business information and technology (Wu and Guo, 2010).

6.3. The Formal Institutional Change and the Development of Shaoxing Textile Cluster

6.3.1. *The development of Terephthalic Acid (PTA) industry in China*

The Shaoxing textile cluster hosts some of the most efficient private firms in the synthetic fiber industry in China. Since a relatively complete industrial chain has already been formed in Shaoxing City, some clustered firms have the intention of launching terephthalic acid (PTA) projects in order to make more profits and realize industrial integration further. In 2003, about 10 corporations in China were reported to the National Development and Reform Commission (NDRC) by the Zhejiang Provincial Government to apply for the PTA program (Zhao, 2004). However, only two of them eventually obtained the production licenses. One was Hualian Sunshine Petro-Chemical Co., Ltd. and the other was Oriental Petrochemical (Shanghai) Co., Ltd., which was set up in the Shanghai Pudong New District by Taiwan Far Eastern Textile Co., Ltd. in January 2003.

PTA is the preferred raw material used to manufacture polyethylene terephthalate, a widely used PET polymer for the production of textiles, bottles, packaging and film products (Fig. 6.1). The world output in

Fig. 6.1.   PTA in the synthetic fiber industry.

Source: Compiled by the author.

1970 was around 1.75 million tons. By 2006, the global PTA demand had substantially exceeded 30 million tons. About 90% of PTA production was used in the textile industry in China. The production and consumption of PTA in China ranked the first around the world. In 2005, the output of PTA was 5.89 million tons while the domestic demand reached 12.14 million tons, yet China had to import 6.49 million tons (Xinhua News, 2006).

Para-xylene (PX) is another petroleum-derived raw material used in the manufacture of PET. It is a major polymer that is used as the main constituent of synthetic textile fibers for clothing, thin films for packaging and containers for beverages. About 99% of PX produced is used for PET production, making PX a commodity-scale chemical (Xinhua News, 2006).

The lower stream up to PET was fully developed, but the shortage of PTA supply remained a bottleneck of the PET industrial chain in China. The demand from the textile industry in Shaoxing City, Hangzhou City, Tongxiang City and Ningbo City, all in Zhejiang province and the biggest PTA consumption areas in China, was very high, but most of the PTA was mainly imported from abroad. However, the domestic production of PTA and PET was constrained by the administrative system in China. Originally the state-owned China Petroleum & Chemical Corporation (SINOPEC) and CNPC monopolized the production of PTA. Despite advanced technology, huge investment and complex approval procedures, many clustered textile firms attempted to enter the field.

As Table 6.2 indicates, the enterprises that have already launched and undertaken PTA projects include the subsidiaries of SINOPEC, CNPC and some foreign-invested enterprises. British Petroleum (BP) Zhuhai Chemical Limited, located in Zhuhai, a harbor city in Guangdong province, South China, launched its first PTA joint venture with 85% of the capital held by BP and 15% held by Fu Hua Group Ltd., a local company on 9 September 2003. The second PTA plant, the world's largest single train PTA unit, was completed in November 2008. The chemical plant,

Table 6.2. The main producers of PTA in China in 2012.

SINOPEC	Yangzi Petrochemical Shareholding Co., Ltd., Jiangsu Province
	Yizhen Synthetic Fibre Shareholding Co., Ltd., Jiangsu Province
	Luoyang Petrochemical Shareholding Co., Ltd., Henan Province
	Shanghai Petrochemical Shareholding Co., Ltd., Shanghai City
	Tianjin Petrochemical Shareholding Co., Ltd., Tianjin City
CNPC	Liaoyang Petrochemical Fiber Company, Liaoning Province
FIEs	BP Zhuhai Chemical Limited, Guangdong Province
	Xiamen Xianglu Petrochemical Co., Ltd., Fujian Province
	Oriental Petrochemical Co., Ltd., Shanghai City
	Ningbo Mitsubishi Chemical Co., Ltd., Zhejiang Province

Source: Compiled by the author.

with a total investment of over USD660 million, had a combined capacity of 1.5 million tons of PTA (BP, 2009).

6.3.2. *The entry of private textile firms in the PTA industry*

Since the PTA program is capital- and technology-intensive, the cost of obtaining patents is very high. Additionally, the project was not allowed to be launched until NDRC and the State Council issued the necessary production licenses. Although some textile firms in the cluster possessed abundant capital and advanced technology, they did not want to expose themselves to high risks because PTA is inflammable and explosive. Those firms that are not engaged in the petro-chemical and oil industries must spend at least two years applying for official licenses.

That the import dependency of PTA was high in China was mainly caused by imperfect competition within the domestic market. The production of PTA was almost totally dominated by the SOEs and FIEs, and the PTA market was not opened to the domestic private firms completely. As some private firms in the Shaoxing textile cluster moved towards the upper stream of industrial chain, the strict market entry barrier made industrial development more difficult. The following is about how the private firms in Shaoxing textile cluster have participated in the PTA industry and how the textile firms have been restructured in the upgrading of textile cluster in the deepening globalization.

Zhejiang Hualian Sunshine Petro-Chemical Co., Ltd. (Hualian Sunshine) was founded at Bing Hai Industrial Park in Shaoxing County in March 2003. It was a large-scale petroleum enterprise with registered capital of RMB970 million. The total assets were RMB8.8 billion and the sales income was RMB2.9 billion from January to September 2006. It was mainly engaged in PTA, PET slices, synthetic fibers and other raw materials. Hualian Sunshine Petro-Chemical Co., Ltd. was the first large-scale state-holding petro-chemical company with private equity participation. The company was jointly invested by the state-owned China Union Holdings Ltd. (51%), and two private enterprises in shaoxing textile cluster including Zhejiang Prospect Industrial Group Limited (24.5%) and Zhejiang Gabriel Industrial Group (24.5%) (Hualian Sunshine, 2006).

China Union Holdings Ltd. is owned by the Union Developing Group of China (UDC) with its headquarter in Shenzhen City. It is a large-scale SOE engaged in the textile and clothing industry under the direct control of central government. It has diversified its business including hi-tech, commerce, trade, finance, real estate and so on. Two subsidiaries of the group have been listed on Shenzhen Stock Exchange, *Hua Lian Kong Gu* and *Shen Zhong Guan*. The group was ranked 280th out of the 1,000 largest enterprise groups of China in 2000 (China Union Holdings Ltd., 2004).

Zhejiang Prospect Industrial Group Limited is a diversified company specializing in PTA, synthetic fiber, soy protein fiber, dyeing and finishing of textile products, automobile spare parts and international trade. It owns seven subsidiaries and holds shares in three other companies. The company, which was listed on the Growth Enterprise Market of Hong Kong Stock Exchange on 18th February 2004, was named one of "The most profitable large-scale enterprises in China" by the central government, one of the "Top 50 enterprises in Shaoxing" by the local government and amongst the "Top 100 potential enterprises in China" by Forbes in 2005 (Zhejiang Prospect Industrial Group Limited, 2007).

Zhejiang Gabriel Industrial Group (Gabriel) was established in Shaoxing County in 2001 with registered capital of RMB260 million. Zhejiang Yong Long Enterprise Co., Ltd. one of the subsidiaries of Gabriel, was listed on the Growth Enterprise Market, Hong Kong Stock Exchange on 8 November 2002. It was the first private textile company from the mainland that was listed on Hong Kong Stock Exchange. The group developed itself from a sole textile company into a large-scale investment company specializing in textiles, garments, dyeing, petrochemical, real estate, investment and international trade (Gabriel, 2007).

Hualian Sunshine Petro-Chemical Co., Ltd. started up its new PTA plant with annual output of 600,000 tons in Shaoxing County in 2005. The new facility was the first to use Eastman Chemical Co. PTA technology (EPTA) from the United States, developed through an alliance with Lurgi Oel Gas Chemie, Frankfurt am Main, Germany and SK Chemicals, South Korea. The alliance forged by Eastman and Lurgi with its cooperation partner SK Chemicals formed a strong association that provided expertise in the fields of engineering, technology, production and processing to final products. PTA was produced in the plant 24 months after the order was awarded to Lurgi. This PTA project was one of the largest single line productions in the world and was constructed in the shortest period. Compared with the conventional PTA technology, the EPTA process offers the advantages of lower investment costs as well as substantially lower production costs (China Union Holdings Ltd., 2004).

6.3.3. *The second phase of the PTA program of Hualian Sunshine Petro-Chemical Co., Ltd.*

The macro-economic adjustments of the central government in 2004 resulted in entirely different fates for the private firms in the Shaoxing textile cluster. The PTA program of Zhejiang Zongheng Light Textile Group had to be stopped because of the shortage of capital caused by the macro-economic adjustment policies adopted by the central government. After negotiating for more than one month, Hualian Sunshine Petro-Chemical Co., Ltd. agreed to purchase the production line.

The PTA project was submitted to the provincial government at the beginning of 2003, but it was not subsequently reported to the NDRC. However, Zhejiang Zongheng Light Textile Group had started to negotiate with foreign companies at the end of 2002 and the project was initiated at the beginning of 2003. Before transferring the project, the company had already signed the equipment purchase contract with E.I. du Pont de Nemours Company of the United States. The project, which was advanced in technology and rich in scientific content, was not designated as "over-investment" by the central government. Since the license was not standardized, the project had to be suspended on 26 April 2004 because the relevant application procedures were not complete (Li, 2004).

When Zhejiang Zongheng Light Textile Group was in trouble, Hualian Sunshine Petro-Chemical Company sent out rescue signals with the support and coordination of the local government. In September 2003, Hualian Sunshine Petro-Chemical Company obtained a formal license to construct the first-phase of a 60-ton PTA program with an investment of RMB2.4 billion. The objective of Hualian Sunshine Petro-Chemical Company was to have the capacity to produce 200,000 tons of PTA within two to three years. The negotiation of restructuring was smooth as a result of mutual concessions. Yet, after the two companies signed the agreement, Hualian Sunshine Petro-Chemical Company still had to wait for the approval of the State Council.

In fact, the government officials of NDRC visited Zhejiang province in June 2004 and held discussions with local officials to find a solution to the illegal PTA projects. However, they did not make any comments since the local government officials hoped that the projects could continue. Ningbo Municipal Government approved the PTA project of the Yisheng Group; the PTA project of Zongheng Group was approved by Zhejiang Economic and Trade Committee. NDRC did not care much about the restructuring of enterprises, but the implementation of PTA programs needed to go through the complete procedures to obtain the licenses. Otherwise, the banks were not allowed to grant the loans to the project (Li, 2004).

The board of directors of China Union Holdings Ltd. issued an announcement to take over the PTA program with annual output of 600,000 tons from Zhejiang Zong Heng Group on 25 August 2005. The project was approved by NDRC on 21 December 2005 and it became the second-phase of the PTA program at Shaoxing Industrial Development Zone. The total investment of the second-phase PTA program was as high as RMB222 million (Chen, 2005).

After the second-phase of the PTA project was completed and implemented in October 2006, the output of Hualian Sunshine Petro-Chemical Co., Ltd. reached 1.5 million tons annually. It became the first PTA producer in the world owning two sets of the latest PTA production lines, promoting the extension of the textile industry in Shaoxing City to the upper stream petrochemical industry at that time (UDC Group, 2006).

Table 6.3. The financing of Hualian Sunshine Petro-Chemical Co., Ltd. through mutual guarantee from 2007–2009.

Mutually guaranteed corporations	Amount of banking loans	Duration
Jinggong Holding Group	RMB3 billion	2 years
Nan Fang Group	RMB6 billion	2 years
Ci Fu Corporation	RMB7 billion	2 years
Yuan Dong Group	RMB8 billion	2 years
Total	RMB24 billion	

Source: UNDC Group (2007).

On 6 March 2007, China Union Holdings Ltd. announced that it planned to reduce the guaranteed quota for Hualian Sunshine after the bank loans became due. The financing of Hualian Sunshine Petro-Chemical Co., Ltd., which was previously guaranteed by the three share-holding companies, changed into the guarantee by the textile firms in Shaoxing textile cluster to purchase the PTA from it. The renewal and added bank loans of Hualian Sunshine through mutual guarantee by the clustered firms amounted to RMB240 billion in 2007, providing the cash flow for the PTA project (UDC Group, 2007).

Except Jinggong Holding Group, which is mainly engaged in steel structure construction and real estate, Nan Fang Group, Ci Fu Corporation and Yuan Dong Group were the textile firms in Shaoxing Textile Cluster that had business transactions with Hualian Sunshine Petro-Chemical Co., Ltd. (Table 6.3). The state-owned Zhejiang Yuan Dong Group was one of 26 key large-scale enterprise groups in Zhejiang province. Zhejiang Yuan Dong New PET Co., Ltd., Shaoxing Bing Hai Petro-Chemical Co., Ltd. and Zhejiang Yuan Dong Chemical Fiber Co., Ltd. were its core subsidiaries.

6.3.4. *The impacts of global financial crisis on the PTA industry in Shaoxing Textile Cluster*

In 2008, the demands for textile and clothing products were plunged in Europe and the United States under the global financial crisis. Accordingly, it resulted in a downturn in the demand for PTA in China. Due to the bad management and cyclical fluctuations, Hualian Sunshine Petro-Chemical Co., Ltd. went bankrupt in September 2008. As a result, both Zhejiang Prospect Industrial Group Limited and Zhejiang Gabriel Group suffered from considerable loss. Four subsidiaries of Zhejiang Gabriel Group went bankrupt while its listed subsidiaries, Zhejiang Yong Long Enterpries Company Ltd. was acquired by Yong Li Group in October 2010. Zhejiang Prospect Industrial Group Limited Undertook overall restructuring (Luo, 2011). Shaoxing County Municipal Government took quick actions to bail out the leading petro-chemical company in the region. Zhejiang Yuandong Chemical Fiber Group and Shaoxing County Bing Hai Industrial District Development and Investment Co., Ltd. acquired Hualian Sunshine Petro-Chemical Co., Ltd. in October 2008 with the coordination of Shaoxing County Municipal Government (China Union Holdings Ltd., 2009). Hualian Sunshine Petro-Chemical Co., Ltd. was renamed Yuandong Petro-Chemical Co., Ltd. The first production line resumed working at the beginning of November 2008 (Li, 2009).

Under the global financial crisis, the central government of China issued new policies to stimulate domestic demands and implemented a series of favorable policies to promote the development of textiles and clothing industry, such as textile industry restructuring and revitalization plan in early 2009. In addition, the central government raised the export tax rebate rate to make Chinese textiles and clothing products more competitive in the international market (Department of Commerce of Zhejiang Province, 2011). A lot of textile and clothing enterprises begun to target the domestic market As a consequence, the demands for PTA recovered and its price went up steadily. With the recovery of PTA market, the sales volume of Yuandong Petro-Chemical Co., Ltd. reached RMB16 billion in 2010 (Luo, 2011).

6.4. Ownership Change of China Textile City and the Development of Shaoxing Textile Cluster

In addition to stimulating and coordinating the industrial development, Shaoxing Municipal Government has been taking an active part in developing the local specialized textile market to promote the development, upgrading and internationalization of Shaoxing textile cluster. The formation and growth of Shaoxing textile cluster is closely related to China Textile City. Zhejiang China Light & Textile Industrial City Group Co., Ltd., which manages China Textile City, is mainly engaged in the development of specialized textile markets as well as the production and marketing of textiles, chemicals and construction raw materials. Before the Initial Public Offering (IPO) of A shares on the Shanghai Stock Exchange, the total equity of Zhejiang China Light & Textile Industrial City Group amounted to RMB87.75 million. On 8 January 1997, CSRC announced that the Zhejiang China Light & Textile Industrial City Group Co., Ltd. was allowed to make its IPO of 29.25 million shares. The company was listed on the Shanghai Stock Exchange successfully on 17 January 1997 and the shares were traded for the first time on 28 February 1997. Since then, Zhejiang China Light & Textile Industrial City Group has been promoting the development and internationalization of Shaoxing textile cluster through public financing with the firm support of the local government. The relationship between the public sector and the private sector has witnessed the dynamic change in the course of cluster development since the growth of the Shaoxing textile cluster has been closely related to the equity changes of the Zhejiang China Light & Textile Industrial City Group in the following decade.

6.4.1. The privatization of China Textile City during 2002–2006

China Textile City originates from a cloth street to one of the biggest specialized textile markets in China. However, it experienced some investment failures in the capital market in 2002, which made the listed company suffer from a huge loss because of falsification of accounts by Yin Guang Sha (000557), another listed company at Shanghai Stock Exchange and led to the equity change of the listed company. In September 2002, Shaoxing Cai Hong Industrial Corporation, which was a state-owned company and the biggest shareholder of Zhejiang China Light & Textile Industrial City Group Co., Ltd., undertook the shareholding reform. Its equity, including 33,679,358 promoter's shares and 14,056,522 public corporate shares were transferred to four legal persons including Jinggong Group Co., Ltd. (see Table 6.4).

Table 6.4. The first 10 shareholders of Zhejiang China Light & Textile Industrial City Group Co., Ltd. in the year 2004.

Shareholders	Quantity of shares	Ratio of total equity (percent)
Zhejiang Jinggong Holding Group Co., Ltd.	47,735,910	12.84
Zhejiang Yong Li Industrial Group Co., Ltd.	29,206,406	7.85
Shaoxing County State-owned Assets Investment and Operation Co., Ltd.	13,275,639	3.57
Zhejiang Financial Development Company	9,136,768	2.46
Fu Guo Dong Tai Ping Heng Security Investment Fund	7,277,297	1.98
Yu Yang Security Investment Fund	5,985,708	1.61
Hongjian Village Committee, Kejiao Village, Shaoxing County	5,154,072	1.39
Shaoxing City Yue Tong Real Estate Company	4,295,061	1.16
Shaoxing County Yin Xiang Economic and Industrial Company	3,092,443	0.83
Jinxin Securities Investment Fund	2,824,049	0.76

Source: Zhejiang China Light & Textile Industrial City Group Co., Ltd. (2004).

It meant that the specialized textile trading market was privatized. On 24 January 2006, Shaoxing County State-owned Assets Investment and Operation Co., Ltd. transferred the remaining 13,275,639 corporate shares to Zhejiang Jinggong Holding Group Co., Ltd. Zhejiang Yong Li Industrial Group Co., Ltd. also transferred all of their shares to the biggest shareholder, owning 26.11% shares of the listed company in the year 2006. Jinggong Holding Group, one private enterprise in Shaoxing City, became the overall controller of the listed company (Fig. 6.2).

Jinggong Holding Group, listed among China's largest 1,000 enterprise groups, is mainly engaged in aviation, steel building, real estate, automobiles and machinery, and Shaoxing rice wine. It was originally Shaoxing County Yangxunqiao Comprehensive Processing Factory established in 1968, a collective enterprise mainly specialized in handicrafts. The factory, embarking on the manufacturing of small farming machines in 1972, was renamed

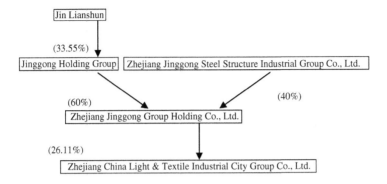

Fig. 6.2. The property rights and the last controller of Zhejiang China Light & Textile Industrial City Group Co., Ltd. in the year 2006.

Source: Zhejiang China Light & Textile Industrial City Group Co., Ltd. (2006).

Yangxunqiao Farm Electromechanical Repair Station. In 1981, it successfully developed the ZJ-2 type of jacquard warp knitters and entered the warp-knitting machinery market. Jin Liangshun was the factory director at that time. The factory undertook one Spark Program project[1] in 1986 and one national Torch Program project[2] in 1989, making great strides in technological progress. Ever since, it has expanded its own business by means of scientific and technological development. The initial accumulation of capital and technology was thus attained. Seizing the opportunities from China's market-oriented reform, the enterprise developed by leaps and bounds. The joint-stock shareholding reform was carried out in 1993. Zhejiang Huang

---

[1] Launched in 1986, the Spark Program aims to revitalize rural economy through science and technology and popularize science and technology in rural areas. There are more than 100,000 scientific and technological demonstration projects being carried out in 85% of rural areas throughout China at present.

[2] Launched in August 1988, Torch Program is China's most important program of high-tech industries. As a guiding program of China, it includes: Organizing and carrying out projects of developing high-tech products with high technological standards and good economic benefits in domestic and foreign markets; establishing some high-tech industrial development zones around China; exploring management systems and operation mechanisms suitable for hi-tech industrial development. The program mainly includes projects in new technological fields, such as new material, biotechnology, electronic information, integrative mechanical-electrical technology, and advanced and energy-saving technology.

Neng Jinggong Group, which was established on 23 January 1996, was honored as a "National Advanced Enterprise in terms of Production Scale and Sound Economic Benefits during the 8th Five-Year Plan". It was renamed Zhejiang Jinggong Holding Group Co., Ltd. in July 1997. In 1999, the Group was transformed into a private shareholding enterprise. In September 2000, Zhejiang Jinggong Science & Technology Co., Ltd. was set up through business restructuring. In September 2002, the group successfully purchased Shaoxing Cai Hong Industrial Corporation and became the largest shareholder of Zhejiang China Light & Textile Industrial City Group Co., Ltd. Jinggong Holding Group was listed in the Top 100 Private Enterprises of Zhejiang Province in 2003. The Jinggong Steel Building Construction Group was listed successfully through purchasing "Chang Jiang Kong Gu" (600496) on the Shanghai Stock Exchange in June 2003. Zhejiang Jinggong Science & Technology Co., Ltd. was also listed successfully on the Shenzhen Stock Exchange, known as "Jinggong Science" (002006) in June 2004 (Jinggong Holding Group, 2006).

After its privatization in 2002, China Textile City was not developed as rapidly as the local government had expected. The gross profits declined sharply from RMB56,938,525.71 in 2003 to RMB −100,517,693.01 in 2006 while the earnings of each share failed to rise steadily and hit the bottom of RMB −0.20 in 2006 (Table 6.5). The sales volume of China Textile City in 2005 could not compete against China Eastern Silk Market in Wujiang City, Jiangsu Province. Meanwhile, about 10 large-scale textile trading markets went into construction in the Yangtze River Delta, including Zhejiang Changxing Light Textile City, Shanghai Yangpu International Textile City, Shanghai Fengjing Clothing City, Jiangsu Wuxi International Textile and Clothing City, Jiangsu Wuxi Oriental International Light Textile City, Jiangsu Wujiang International Textile City, Jiangsu Changshu International Clothing City, Jiangsu Suzhou Xiangchen International Clothing City, Jiangsu China Sutong Light Textile City, Jiangsu Gaoyou Huangshi International Clothing and Textile City and so on since 2003. The newly-built textile trading markets had the late-development advantages and their facilities were far more advanced than China Textile City. Some businessmen in these newly built textile trading markets used to undertake their business at China Textile City. The main reason why they chose to leave was very high business costs there.

Table 6.5. The main financial indicators of Zhejiang China Light & Textile Industrial City Group Co., Ltd. from the year 2002–2006 (Currency: RMB).

Financial indicators	2002	2003	2004	2005	2006
The main business income	1,384,761,083.78	1,399,612,634.81	1,020,766,574.02	839,898,693.45	979,934,924.23
Gross profits	54,971,406.68	56,938,525.71	52,893,116.66	25,588,412.90	−100,517,693.01
Net profits	8,590,083.94	5,312,278.58	21,484,940.51	11,160,145.97	−96,214,072.86
Net profits after extraordinary items	8,343,004.22	−35,993,523.19	2,169,751.39	−5,217,418.26	−111,852,700.66
Earnings of each share	0.023	0.014	0.058	0.030	−0.20
Net assets earnings ratio (%)	0.89	0.54	2.15	1.08	−10.37

Sources: Zhejiang China Light & Textile Industrial City Group Co., Ltd. (2002–2006).

Table 6.6.   The main financial indicators of Zhejiang China Light & Textile Industrial City Group Co., Ltd. from the year 2007–2011 (Currency: RMB).

Financial indicators	2007	2008	2009	2010	2011
The main business income	853,761,088.86	578,412,221.38	281,305,215.38	333,623,024.20	345,846,521.81
Gross profits	211,450,331.91	133,659,049.46	68,648,234.52	20,857,294.20	152,183,330.16
Net profits	138,945,330.78	72,155,082.03	69,000,139.38	40,427,197.55	123,498,658.57
Net profits after extraordinary items	65,999,725.82	68,159,831.61	61,501,525.23	68,443,532.30	105,473,524.88
Earnings of each share	0.29	0.12	0.11	0.07	0.20
Net assets earnings ratio (%)	13.55	6.27	6.31	3.16	9.09

Sources: Zhejiang China Light & Textile Industrial City Group Co., Ltd. (2006–2011).

After China Textile City was wholly privatized in 2002, the rent of business booths within the textile trading market skyrocketed. The bidding for the rent of one business booth with 30 square meters for six years reached RMB3.8 million without any installments. The rent was 5–10 times higher than the initial transfer. Because landlords could enjoy high rents, there were more and more "sub-contracted" landlords in the textile trading market. In addition, the supporting facilities there were lagging behind, with little systematic or scientific planning. The general image of the market was obsolete (Ruan *et al.*, 2006).

6.4.2. *The re-emergence of the local government*

Market mechanisms alone were unable to coordinate the frenzied and speculative trading of the business booths within the China Textile City efficiently. The deficiency of market mechanism needed to be complemented by regulation and control from the local government. Thus, in April 2006, "*Various Suggestions on Developing China Light Textile City*" was issued by Shaoxing County Municipal Government. It specified that China Textile City would be developed into an "International Textile Capital". Meanwhile, Keqiao City would be developed into "A City of Modern Business and Commerce" through nurturing tertiary industries on the basis of specialized textile market (China Textile City, 2013).

Therefore, Shaoxing County Municipal Government negotiated with Jinggong Holding Group on the equity transfer of specialized textile market in 2006. Jinggong Group signed an agreement of intention with Shaoxing County Municipal Government that it intended to transfer 72,694,114 shares to Shaoxing China Textile City Development and Construction Company, which was established by Shaoxing County State-owned Assets Investment and Operation Company in June 2003. China Textile City was included in the overall planning of Shaoxing County Municipal Government.

In order to avoid the depreciation of previous storefront or booth owners within China Textile City after the local government took over the textile trading market, differential strategies were applied to the renovation of Shaoxing textile trading market. The new generation of textile trading market was not simply replicating, but complementing the old generation of market. For example, the local government invested RMB2 million to renovate and expand the market from the previous 600,000 square meters to 1.6 million square meters in 2006. The newly-added one million meters, consisting of the south and north markets, were wholly controlled by the local government. The specialized trading market, which was owned by Jingong Group, became part of south market. It was not separated in the overall plans. After the completion of the new development, the south market mainly deals in cloth while the north market trades in textile products. In October 2008, Shaoxing County Municipal Government formally acquired Zhejiang China Light & Textile Industrial City Group Co., Ltd. from Zhejiang Jinggong Group and became the majority shareholder of management company (China Textile City, 2013). With the equity transfer, Shaoxing textile trading market is able to enjoy more favorable policies from the local government in terms of tax exemptions and improvements in the business environment.

Shaoxing County Municipal Government has issued a series of favorable policies to attract new entrants and encourage new businesses in the newly-built textile trading market in terms of tax, rent, export rebates and so on. In particular, the new entrants could enjoy the most favorable rents for business booths within the market. When the businesses entered the united market and Qianqing Raw Material Market before 31 October 2008, the annual rent of standardized business stores lay between RMB10,000–20,000 in the first two years. The daily rent of business stores in the new international trade district was between RMB0.8–2.5 per square meter. The businesses that entered the new generation of textile trading market before 31 October 2008 could sign a five-year contract and enjoy the rent exemption in the first two years. The rent in the following three years was subject to the business transactions of new generation of textile trading market (China Textile City Construction and Management Committee, 2013). Since August 2008, Shaoxing City Municipal Government has been striving to upgrade the textile cluster and build the region into an international textile manufacturing, trading and creation center.

6.5. Conclusion

The development of Shaoxing textile cluster has shown that the private textile firms usually need to cooperate with the SOEs when they move up the value chain. The participation in the capital-intensive PTA industry is a typical example in promoting the vertical integration of synthetic fiber industry in Shaoxing textile cluster. An effective partnership with the SOEs allows private entrepreneurs to acquire capital, technology and essential licenses of entry into the PTA industry. The partnership can not only help private textile firms meet the changes of regulatory framework, but also manage business risks more effectively. By forming an alliance with the state-owned China Union Holdings Ltd., the two private firms in Shaoxing textile cluster obtained the PTA production licenses from NDRC and enter the capital-intensive petro-chemical industry successfully. With the firm support of local government, Hualian Sunshine Petro-Chemical Co., Ltd. was restructured successfully by other State-owned firms in the textile cluster with the coordination of local government under the global financial crisis.

The equity change of Zhejiang China Light & Textile Industrial City Group Co., Ltd. from the public to private in 2002 led to the development of the market being brought to a standstill in 2004. The main reason was that the local government of Shaoxing County ceded their dominant role in the development and upgrading of the textile trading market. The local government plays an important role in correcting market failure and fostering the long-term planning of China Textile City. Thus, in 2006, Shaoxing County Municipal Government re-emerged as an important player in the development of China Textile City, alongside the private shareholders. The effective combination between the local government control and market power has proved to create a better commercial environment and reduce the business costs of the specialized textile trading market.

The development of SME textile cluster in Shaoxing City has demonstrated that the local state continues to play a significant role in the institution-building process of regional development. As one important institutional arrangement, the specialized textile trading market has contributed greatly to the formation, growth and internationalization of local textile cluster.

7

YIWU SOCKS CLUSTER

7.1. Introduction

As a county-level city located in the middle part of Zhejiang province, Yiwu has an area of 1,105 square kilometers with a permanent population of 1.23 million in 2012. The population with local household registration is around 640,000 while the population with migrant household registration is around 590,000. There are six towns and seven sub-districts in its jurisdiction. In 1988, Yiwu County was changed into Yiwu City. Since China's adoption of the open-door policy in 1978, Yiwu City has been implementing the strategy of developing the city through promoting commerce and fostering a market system on the basis of commodities trade, thereby promoting regional economic development and realizing a historic transition from a traditional agricultural county to a prosperous modern commercial city. The GDP reached RMB80.294 in 212 (National Bureau of Statistics of Yiwu, 2013). Yiwu City has become one of the biggest distribution and exhibition centers of small commodities around the world (Yiwu Municipal Government, 2013). Although it suffered from the global financial crisis in 2008 and 2009, the turnover of Yiwu Commodity Trading Market reached RMB58.03 billion in 2012 (CCC Group, 2013) (see Table 7.1). Some industrial clusters have emerged and developed rapidly including socks, ornaments, zippers, shirts, and handicrafts on the basis of commodity trading market (Jin *et al.*, 2010, Bellandi and Lombardi, 2012).

Yiwu City has become one of the most important socks production bases in China. Yiwu socks' cluster has come into being and witnessed a rapid development. The output of silk socks, cotton socks and panty-hoses

Table 7.1. The turnover of Yiwu Commodity Trading Market in 2001–2012 (RMB100 million).

Year	Turnover	Percentage change %
2001	212.0	9.8
2002	230.0	8.5
2003	248.3	8.0
2004	266.9	7.5
2005	288.5	8.1
2006	315.0	9.2
2007	348.4	10.6
2008	381.8	9.6
2009	411.6	7.8
2010	456.1	10.8
2011	515.1	12.9
2012	580.0	12.6

Source: CCC Group (2013).

reached 5 billion pairs with a sales volume hitting RMB6 billion, accounting for 40% of total output of those commodities in China in 2006. The annual income of leading socks enterprises including Yiwu Langsha Socks Co., Ltd., Yiwu Mengna Socks Co., Ltd., Yiwu Fenli Socks Co., Ltd. and Yiwu Baonas Socks Co., Ltd. surpassed RMB100 million (Yiwu Commmercial News, 2006). In 2011, the sales turnover of hosiery industry in Yiwu City reached RMB12.5 billion and the export value hit USD700 million, accounting for 15.8% of total in the city (Yiwu Municipal Government, 2012).

7.2. Informal Institutions and the Development of Yiwu Socks Cluster

The majority of entrepreneurs in Yiwu socks cluster originate from the grassroots in rural areas. They started their socks businesses from scratch. Yiwu is not rich in natural resources, but the local people have traditionally been sensitive to market opportunities and have the courage to put their business plans into practice. The local people have, since the Qing dynasty, a long tradition of peddling and selling brown sugar in exchange for rooster feathers around the neighboring rural areas. At the beginning of the 1980s, some entrepreneurs began to pursue their peddling business across a wider area in China, contributing to the spatial expansion of the local commodity trading market and the dramatic increase of domestic socks sales. Others became booth-keepers at the local commodity trading market, engaged in the introduction of products manufactured in various industrial clusters along the coastal provinces, mainly in Zhejiang province and Guangdong province, to the rest of China (Zhang, 1993).

Social network plays an important part in the formation and development of Yiwu socks cluster, which indicates a strong feature of flexible specialization. The local industrial network is mainly woven by households, neighbors, relatives and friends on the basis of siblings, kinships and regional contacts. Thousands of small- and medium-sized socks firms are scattered in the rural areas of Yiwu City, specializing in different stages of socks production, including knitting, dyeing, shaping, packaging, marketing, supply of raw materials, sales and maintenance of knitting machinery. Family members, relatives, friends and neighbors share the different processes of socks production. The inter-firm network on the basis of social network is critical for the survival and growth of most socks firms in the cluster. The small- and medium-sized socks firms have developed horizontal and vertical business linkages in the production of intermediate and finished socks through social network. They forecast market trends, exchange production and management experiences together, complete large orders and increase their bargaining power together (Wang, 2011).

Most of socks firms in the cluster are family workshops. The family members usually offer financial support for the new venture creation. When the socks enterprise is established, they usually take an active part in running the business. For example, Langsha Group has grown from a small socks agent into one of the leading socks' enterprises in China. At the beginning of the 1990s, three brothers entered into the development, production and sales of socks and knitting underwear together. Rongjin Weng, general manager of Langsha Group, worked as an agent for a socks company in Guangdong province, South China. His business became one of the biggest at Yiwu Commodity Trading Market in 1995. Its marketing network covered the whole China, which contributed to the rapid growth of company later on. After finishing the initial capital accumulation, Rongjin Wen decided to set up its own socks manufacturing company after realizing that Yiwu City would become one of the main socks manu-facturing and marketing centers in China with the rapid development of local commodity trading market (Xu, 2006).

Langsha Group aims to become one of the leading international socks producers. In 2000, its brand reputation, market share and pro-duction scale were ranked first in the socks industry throughout China. The "Langsha" was listed as one of the famous brands in China by the State Industrial and Commercial Bureau on 8 February 2002 (Jia and Sun, 2004). Langsha Group has been trying to international-ize its own brand. There are not many socks firms in China, which are promoting their products in the overseas market with their own brands. Most of socks exports in China have been mainly made through OEM. The socks companies in the cluster have realized that they need to learn the demands and tastes of overseas consumers more deeply, respond to the market changes more quickly and conduct international marketing more efficiently.

Langsha Group has adopted a diversification strategy to become a busi-ness group covering socks, underwear, cosmetics, medicine and invest-ment. Langsha Group Holding Co., Ltd. was established in April 2005 with registered capital of RMB70 million. It was mainly a family business when it was established. Guangrong Wen, who owns 33.33% of the equity, works as general manager of Langsha Knitting Company and deputy general manager of Langsha Group Holding. Rongjin Wen, who owns 33.34% of the equity, acts as chairman of board of Hong Guang Knitting Company, Langsha Knitting Company and executive director of Langsha Group Holding; Rongdi Wen, who owns 33.33% of Langsha Group Holding, works as chairman of board of Langsha underwear com-pany and Langsha cosmetics company, general manager of Langsha Group Holding and Hong Guang Knitting Company (see Fig. 7.1). The core enterprises include Langsha Underwear Company and Langsha Knitting Company. Langsha Knitting Company was established in 1995 with registered capital of RMB14.6 million, among which Hong Guang Knitting Company holds 51% equity and Langsha International Company

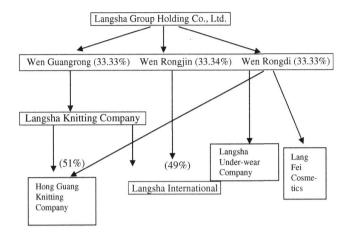

Fig. 7.1. The organization of Langsha Group Holding Co., Ltd.
Source: Langsha (2008).

owns 49% equity. Langsha Underwear Company was established in 2006 with registered capital of RMB6.6 million. The main business is the making and marketing of knitting underwear products. The other subsidiaries include Hong Guang Knitting Company, Langsha International Company, Shanghai Langsha Company, Langsha Real Estate Company, Langfei Cosmetics Company, Langsha Tuopu Company, Lifu Textiles and Knitting Company. Shanghai Langsha mainly deals in the marketing of knitting and textile products, daily necessities and cosmetics. Langsha Cosmetics is engaged in the production and marketing of washing powder, perfumes, shampoo and skin-care products. The business scope of Lifu Textiles and Knitting Company includes the production and marketing of synthetic fabrics. More and more socks enterprises in the cluster have started to implement diversification strategies to extend their production lines, expand their businesses and improve their competitiveness in the domestic and international market (Langsha, 2008).

With the rapid development of the capital market, more and more private firms in China wanted to be listed to reduce their costs of financing. However, there were (and still are) quota restrictions stipulated by CSRC on the number of IPOs in any one year. Thus, some entrepreneurial private firms, including Langsha Group, had to make the direct financing from the capital market by taking over some poorly-performing listed company at

Shanghai Stock Exchange or Shenzhen Stock Exchange. Langsha Group was listed at Shanghai Stock Exchange on 1 September 2006 by acquiring the state-owned Sichuan Changjiang Packaging Holding Co., Ltd. (ST Chang Kong) with headquarters in Yibing City, Sichuan Province (Langsha, 2009).

7.3. The Local Government, Commodity Trading Market and the Development of Yiwu Socks Cluster

The formation and development of Yiwu socks cluster are closely linked to Yiwu Commodity Trading Market, which is currently the world's largest market. The development of Yiwu Commodity Trading Market has been completely dominated by the local government. Yiwu Municipal Government has played an important part in the establishment, development and internationalization of commodity trading market, leading to the rapid growth and upgrading of Yiwu socks cluster. The commodity trading market has moved to five locations and undertaken nine major expansions under the direction of the local government in the past three decades (see Table 7.2). Yiwu Municipal Government faced risks and challenges at each expansion and transition of commodity trading market. However, it made effective reform and innovation of local public administrative system to meet the rapid regional development revolving around the commodity trading market.

Table 7.2. The evolution of Yiwu commodity trading market during 1982–2012.

Generation of commodity trading market	Year	Location
The first generation	1982–1983	Huqing Gate, Choucheng Town (county town), Niansanli Town
The second generation	1984–1985	Xinma Road, Choucheng Town
The third generation	1986–1991	Chengzhong Road, Choucheng Town
The fourth generation	1992–2001	Huangyuan market, Bingwan market, at Choucheng Town
The fifth generation	2002–present	Huangyuan market, Bingwan market and International Trade City, at Choucheng Town

Source: Wang and Ngoasong (2012).

7.3.1. *Improve the allocation of market resources with effective use of administrative means*

The launch of the commodity trading market by Yiwu Municipal Government in 1982 was a risky decision since Chinese farmers were strictly prohibited from undertaking any commercial activities at that time. The local government officials were confronted with political risks if they supported the small commodity market in the street openly because street markets were against the planned economy and beyond the control by the local and national government. Yiwu Municipal Government held several meetings to explore the future of the street market, but failed to reach any consensus because none of senior local government officials dared to assume the political risks of supporting capitalism openly. In April 1982, Gaohua Xie was assigned to work as party secretary of Yiwu Municipal Government. He bravely took personal responsibility for the decision to support the growth of small commodity market (Xie, 1997; Gao and Feng, 2008). Later, the local government put forward the *"Four Permissions"* and *"Five Supports"*, which provided a shortcut for economic development in Yiwu City. The farmers in Yiwu City were allowed to undertake four types of business activity, namely, engaging in commerce in the urban area, undertaking long-distance logistics, competing with state-owned enterprises and opening up the commodity trading market. Afterwards, the informal markets on the urban streets were replaced by one regular commodity trading market in a special transaction area. The commodity trading market expanded its scale to accommodate more than 5,500 booths in 1986. It became the largest one of its kind with the widest diffusion in China at the beginning of 1990s (Ding, 2006).

In the first 10 years after the market was established, its organization, operation and management were dealt with mainly by the Yiwu Industrial and Commercial Bureau affiliated with Yiwu Municipal Government. Zhejiang Yiwu China Commodities City Shareholding Co., Ltd. (Yiwu China Commodities City) was established in 1993, with Haonan Fang, Yiwu's mayor as chairman of the board after the local government decided to transform the operating system and implement the strategy of "Developing the city through prospering commerce" (Yiwu Commercial News, 2008).

Yiwu was the first city to separate management from ownership of the commodity trading market in 1994. This transformation of the operating system at Yiwu China Commodities City took place three years earlier than equivalent transformations across the rest of China. Yiwu China Commodities City was principally responsible for market construction and development, the maintenance of market order and the undertaking of property management. An industrial and commercial sub-bureau, a police unit, a national tax bureau and a local tax bureau were established within the commodity trading market, their respective enforcement powers delegated by Yiwu Municipal Government. As a result, the market environment was improved considerably. Once any conflicts arose, Yiwu Municipal Government would intervene to coordinate the various bureaus and ensure the orderly and smooth development of the market as a whole (He, 2005). In contrast, at some other commodity trading markets in China, different departments of local government were given responsibility for managing market development, and the resulting rivalry amongst those departments often led to the abuse of administrative power, which was counterproductive to further market development. Yiwu Municipal Government, on the other hand, adopted a business model of managing the commodity trading market through one single entity.

This commodity trading market played an important role in stimulating local economic development, so Yiwu Municipal Government established a new Market Development Bureau in 1999, responsible for market planning and development to promote an orderly and smooth development of the market as a whole. In addition, it also sets up the Construction Supervision Department of the International Trade City, a fifth generation market, and sent one member of the municipal government committee to oversee its construction. This project involved detailed planning, sequential implementation and further development of supporting facilities to allow the market to enjoy an international reputation. After the first district of the International Trade City was opened in 2002, the number of foreign businessmen surged and international trade increased dramatically. By the end of 2008, the International Trade City had been expanded to cover 3 million square meters with 40,000 business booths (Yiwu Commercial News, 2008).

The rent of each booth at the commodity trading market has been guided and stipulated by the local municipal government. Industrial and commercial administrative expenses have been charged only at cost, with national and local taxes levied according to the regulations. The booths on the commodity trading market can be leased and transferred freely, but they must go through certain procedures. The long-term consistent policies implemented by the local government have fundamentally promoted the stability of the market.

7.3.2. Strengthen the specialization of commodity trading market at different locations and agglomerate the same type of commodities within the same district of the market

At the beginning of the 1990s, Yiwu Industrial and Commercial Bureau noticed that the business of several booths engaged in the same type of commodity in the commodity trading market, were especially thriving. They realized that the clustering of the same type of commodities within the same district of the market could attract more business and make the commodity price of the same type more comparable and competitive. Afterwards, Yiwu Industrial and Commercial Bureau undertook a mandatory classification of industries at the commodity trading market (Ke, 2006). At the beginning, some booth keepers objected to these rules since they thought that profit margins would be much thinner if commodities of the same type were put together in the same district and prices became more transparent. Under the circumstances, Yiwu Industrial and Commercial Bureau, which is affiliated with the local government, intervened to maintain the market order. It took five years before all of the booth keepers finally accepted the new state of affairs. Clustering the same type of commodities into one district further strengthened market competition. In addition, classifying industries into specific commodity trading markets at different locations added to the convenience of clients greatly, who are able to compare the price, quality, style of commodities and reputation of booth keepers within the same district more easily before they make their purchases (Lu *et al.*, 2003).

7.3.3. *Promote the industrial development and the formation of SME industrial clusters*

Yiwu Municipal Government developed a series of policies to support the local SMEs. In 1991, it implemented a policy of promoting industrial development and commercial prosperity. The businessmen within the commodity trading market were encouraged to set up their own workshops. The rural industrial parks established in 1994 laid a solid foundation for the rapid growth of local clustered firms (He, 2005). There were about 25,000 manufacturers engaged in 20 industries in Yiwu in 2008, including socks, clothing, textiles, ornaments, zippers, handicrafts, pens and printing, which accounted for 40% of the total industrial output of the city. As Table 7.3 indicates, Yiwu City has become one of the national production bases in China for socks, ornaments and zippers. With regard to ornaments, it had over 70% of total market share in China while the figure for handicrafts was over 60%. The output and sales volume of zippers had reached 25% and 35% of the total in China by the end of 2007 (Jin *et al.*, 2007). Industrial clusters of local SMEs have inevitably formed in these industries over the years. Nearly 95% of the entrepreneurs in Yiwu are ex-vendors, who traded in the commodity trading market and switched to manufacturing afterwards (China Daily, 2008a).

Since 2000, Yiwu Municipal Government has been making efforts to promote technological innovation. In 2008, for example, it spent RMB2.71 billion on the technological upgrading of local enterprises. Under the

Table 7.3.   The scale of main industrial clusters in Yiwu City in 2007.

Industrial clusters	Scale	Leading brands
Socks	One of the biggest socks production bases in China	Langsha MengNa
Ornaments	One of three ornament production bases in China, which occupies over 70% market share	Xinguang
Zipper	25% of total output in China	Weihai
Garments	One of four shirts production bases in China	Nengdali
Handicrafts	60% of total output in China	Huahong, Wang Bin

Source: Jin *et al.* (2007).

global financial crisis, the local government provided RMB200 million to help local firms stimulate innovation, adjust products portfolio and increase their added value (China Daily, 2008b). 900 out of 1,400 applications for patents were approved in Yiwu City in the first nine months of 2008, which indicated that technology-oriented firms were playing a more important part in its industrial growth (China Daily, 2008b). Yiwu Municipal Government aims to nurture more hi-tech firms, but a shortage of professional talents has slowed down the pace of hi-tech industry (China Daily, 2008a).

In the long run, industrial upgrading is still one of the biggest challenges the local government and clustered firms are facing. It is one of the high priorities for the local government to encourage and support the local firms to develop more differentiated and value-added products to improve the competitiveness of industrial clusters. The local government has realized the significance of industrial upgrading and carried out a series of reward policies to encourage the development of processing trade.

7.3.4. *Forge local–global linkage of industrial clusters through internationalizing the commodity trading market*

The model of regional development through the commodity trading market has been questioned in China from time to time (Zheng *et al.*, 2003). The commodity trading market in Yiwu is no exception. At the end of 1990s, the domestic competition became extremely fierce in China as the commodity trading markets mushroomed in the Yangtze River Delta, Pearl River Delta and Bohai-rim region (Li & Fung Research Centre, 2006a). The domestic market was saturated and the profit margins were very thin. Yiwu Commodity Trading Market would have lost its competitiveness and gone into decline without adopting a new strategy.

The local government in Yiwu started to include the internationalization strategy in its blueprint in response since the turn of the century. The internationalization strategy has proven to be a success. The local commodity trading market and clustered firms have been integrated into the global value chain (China Daily, 2008b). The commodities have been exported to 215 countries and regions with an annual growth rate of exports by more than 40% since 2000. The volume of international trade

Table 7.4.   The first three export destinations of Yiwu City in 2009.

Main export destinations	Export value (million USD)	Growth rate (%)
EU	470	26.1
The United States	350	21
The United Emirates	150	3.3
Russia	80	−33

Source: National Bureau of Statistics of Yiwu (2009).

from Yiwu exceeded that of domestic trade in 2002. The total number of standard containers exported from Yiwu has exceeded 500,000 since 2005. As Table 7.4 indicates, the exports of Yiwu City to the European Union and the United States reached USD470 million and USD350 million in 2009, increasing by 26.1% and 21% compared with those in 2008. The Middle East remains one of the major export destinations of Yiwu City. The exports to the United Emirates hit USD150 million. However, there was dramatic reduction of exports to Russia, decreasing by 33%. In 2012, the total value of international trade of Yiwu city amounted to USD9.347 billion among which exports reached USD9.005 billion. The developing countries in Asia, Africa and Latin Ameica became its main export destinations. The first three export destinations were changed into Iran, India and Iraq (National Bureau of Statistics of Yiwu, 2013). About 2,124 representative offices of the overseas companies were established and 10,000 foreign businessmen from over 100 countries were living in the city to undertake procurement at the commodity trading market in 2008 (Yiwu Commercial News, 2008). The internationalization of the commodity trading market has not only forged the local–global linkages of local industrial clusters, but also helped the local clustered firms upgrade along the global value chain.

Once again Yiwu Municipal Government has been playing an active role in the internationalization of the commodity trading market by strengthening the latter's role in foreign business management, including the simplification of customs procedures, commodity inspection procedures and other elements of red tape for overseas businessmen residing and operating their business in Yiwu City. In addition, the foreign affairs management and service system in the city has increasingly improved.

The state ministries and commissions, including Ministry of Foreign Affairs, Ministry of Public Security, Supreme Court, China Banking Regulatory Commission and General Administration of Customs, have successively expanded the management jurisdiction over the foreign affairs of Yiwu Municipal Government. Yiwu was the first county-level city in China to open a civil airport and launched direct flights between Yiwu and Hong Kong in 2009 (He, 2009).

However, there are always obstacles in the course of internationalization of Yiwu Commodity Trading Market. Yiwu was affected considerably by the global financial crisis at the end of 2007 and 2008 (Zhong, 2009). Although the total export volume reached USD1.91 billion and increased by 13.9% in 2008, the growth rate decreased by 11% compared with that in the previous year (National Bureau of Statistics of Yiwu, 2009). There was also a huge reduction of foreign direct investment. Only three foreign-funded industrial projects were approved in 2009 with utilizing the foreign capital of USD1.524 million, which reduced by 80.4% compared with that in 2008 (National Bureau of Statistics of Yiwu, 2010). Therefore, the pace of industrial upgrading was hampered within the region. In addition, with the frequent anti-dumping allegations by both developed and developing countries, the exports of some labor-intensive products such as baby carriers, hardware fitting and stuffed toys have reduced.

Under the global financial crisis, some shortcomings of regional development model with the commodity trading market have come to light. The majority commodities on sale at the market are the cheap labor-intensive products with low added value. About 37.4% SMEs suspended their production at the end of 2008 due to the reduction of orders because the commodity trading market mainly exports to the United States, European Union and the Middle East (National Bureau of Statistics of Yiwu, 2009). As the demand decreased within these main destinations, more and more local businesses started to target the domestic market again or penetrate into the new potential markets in Africa and Latin America (Zhong, 2009).

Meanwhile, some businessmen have cloned commodity trading markets in other regions of China and some foreign countries, including Beijing Yiwu Commodity Wholesale Market, Suzhou Yiwu Commodity

Direct Sale Supermarket (Jiangsu Province), Taiyuan Yiwu Commodity Wholesale Market (Shanxi Province), Lanzhou Yiwu Commodity City (Gansu Province), Urumqi Changzheng Wholesale Market (Xinjiang Uygur autonomous region) and China Commodity Town in Dubai and South Africa. These new markets have not only attracted businessmen from Yiwu to open booths, but also encouraged local businessmen to make procurement from Yiwu Commodity Trading Market. The clustered firms in Yiwu City have also contributed to the formation of an international market network (Wang and Ngoasong, 2012).

7.4. Yiwu Model and its Implications for Regional Development in China and South–South Cooperation

Yiwu model is a typical example of rural development in China relying on the constant expansion of commodity trading market. The growth of commodity trading market has stimulated the entrepreneurial activities of local people and led to the flourishing SMEs in the region. It serves as the main distribution channel for the rural SMEs. In turn, the growth of SMEs has contributed to the further expansion of commodity trading market. In addition, the commodity trading market also acts as an independent marketing platform for the enterprises from other parts of China and foreign countries.

Since the 1990s, Yiwu model has influenced the rest of China and other developing countries. Most of the commodity trading markets in other regions of China that have introduced the operation and management model of Yiwu have achieved success. One of the latest typical examples is Suqian Yiwu International Trade City in Jiangsu province, East China. Weigao Liu, board chairman of Zhejiang Fenli Group in Yiwu, had a bold idea of duplicating Yiwu International Trade City in Suqian City in 2001, where he established Jiangsu Feng Na Si Co., Ltd. In 2005, his business plan was firmly supported by Suqian Municipal Government to set up Suqian Yiwu International Trade City with an investment of RMB2.6 billion. The new market follows the operation and management model of Yiwu Commodity Trading Market. In addition, an industrial park was set up to support 200 new entrepreneurs with RMB15 million on the basis of commodity trading market to stimulate industrial development within the region. The current number of business stalls within Suqian Yiwu International Trade City exceeds 5,000 with monthly business turnover surpassing RMB100 million. The majority of businessmen within the market are from the neighboring provinces including Zhejiang, Anhui, Henan and Shangdong provinces (Suqian Daily, 2010). The success of commodity trading market has promoted the regional economic growth in Suqian City by acting as an important trading platform in the rural areas and streamlining the distribution of commodities. With the successful experiences in Jiangsu province, Weigao Liu launched China Kunmin Luo Shi Wang International Trade City in Yunnan province, southwestern China with Yiwu model on 16 December 2009. The new commodity trading market, which is adjacent to the Association of South-eastern Asian Countries, has stimulated the regional development in West China and contribute to deepening China-ASEAN economic ties (Zhejiang Entrepreneurs, 2009). Meanwhile, some of commodity trading markets have become the secondary markets of Yiwu China Commodities Group. They have not only attracted businessmen from Yiwu City to open business stalls, but also forged close business linkages. For example, Tonghua Yiwu Trade and Business City in Jilin Province, North Eastern China, which was opened in January 2010 with an investment of RMB2.5 billion, has formed close business alliance with Yiwu China Commodities Group in terms of logistics, goods supply and market management. Among the 2,000 business booths, about one-third of owners were from Zhejiang Province and Jiangsu Province (Li *et al.*, 2010).

In addition, Yiwu model has promoted the south–south cooperation. Yiwu China Commodities Group has forged close business linkages with commodity trading markets or China Commodity Town in Dubai (United Arab Emirates), South Korea, South Africa and Tanzania (Yiwu Commercial News, 2008). These overseas commodity trading markets have extended the international marketing network for China Commodities Group and SMEs in Yiwu City. According to Yiwu Entry-Exit Administration of the Public Security Bureau, the number of African visitors hit over 34,000 in 2008, doubled compared with that in 2006. African head offices increased from only 1 in 2000 to 255 in

2008 (China Daily, 2010). As a result, Yiwu China Commodity Group has forged closer business ties with some commodity trading markets in Africa such as China Town in South Africa, Kariakor Wholesale Market in Dar-es-Salaam, Tanzania (Wang and Ngoasong, 2012). The surging trade between Yiwu City and African countries has undoubtedly helped to fight against poverty and stimulate industrial development in some African countries.

7.5. Conclusions

The development of Yiwu socks cluster demonstrates that its success has been closely related to the growth and internationalization of Yiwu Commodity Trading Market. The positive interaction between the informal, formal and international institutions has led to the success of socks cluster. The commodity trading market has also become the driving force of internationalization of local SME industrial clusters with the firm support of local government.

The economic reform in China has been a multi-dimensional process of institutional change since 1978 (Qian, 2000; Naughton, 2007). The case study of Yiwu socks cluster illustrates that the economic development has been promoted through active planning, support and policy intervention by the local government from the very beginning. The commodity trading market in Yiwu City can be regarded as a special institutional arrangement that has effectively integrated local government with market mechanisms, contributing to the formation and growth of local SMEs industrial clusters and promoting the rural economic development. The evolution of market structures, the expansion of market size, and the extension of market sequencing have all combined to generate a series of formal institutional change by Yiwu Municipal Government, having far-reaching impacts on the regional development in the rest of China and other developing countries. Its local government has not retreated in the era of globalization as neo-liberal scholars may have assumed. Instead, its governance capacity has been transformed, its forms of management and control reconfigured and its importance enhanced by the forging of local–global linkages as a result of its initiatives. Thus, in this explanation, the local government can serve as a developmental state in market building and industrial development in the era of globalization. However, it has to redefine its role to meet the volatile business environment resulting from global institutional changes. The local government has to constantly strengthen its governance capacity and offer more public services to local SMEs and industrial clusters. The new institution-building of the local state becomes *embedded* in the evolution and internationalization of the local commodity trading market.

The development of SME industrial clusters in Yiwu City has implications for the rural development in other developing countries in the era of globalization. It demonstrates that the national and local state *can* continue to play an important part in economic development, even in rural areas. In addition, the manner in which national and local governments can contribute to economic development relies on the continuous capacity building of the local state to respond to institutional changes and fierce competition imposed by the deepening globalization.

8

CONCLUSIONS

The Chinese society is undergoing unprecedented social and economic reform. This book has focused on one small aspect of this great transformation — the development of textile and clothing clusters in rural China. At present, China is known as the "workshop of the world". This book has examined the institutional dynamics of SME cluster development in a transitional context.

8.1. The Unique Institutional Factors Leading to the Rapid Development of Textile and Clothing Clusters in Rural China

The unique institutional factors leading to the rapid development of textile and clothing clusters in rural China include hybrid ownership, institutional entrepreneurship and the commodity trading market.

8.1.1. *Hybrid ownership*

Hybrid ownership has been one stepping stone to the growth and development of textile and clothing clusters in rural China. The transformation of ownership in China has been a complex process characterized by the emergence of a newly private sector, the gradual privatization of SOEs by the state using various means and the interaction between institutional legacies and state strategies in an uncertain environment leading to the emergence of new organizational forms. There is still a continuum of ownership forms within industrial clusters in rural China, ranging from private forms to public ones. The hybrid ownership usually involves a

149

multiplicity of heterogeneous owners as well as a fuzzy border between public and private forms with the development of interwoven types. When the large-scale state-owned textile and clothing enterprises were restructured in the 1990s, the assets were diluted into new factories and plants. The former SOEs or collective enterprises were usually turned into a joint stock company, but still kept the controlling shares of the new company. The former SOE managers could also buy shares in the new companies or establish their own private firms, integrating them within the holding companies as suppliers or customers.

The case study evidence indicates that the growth of Ningbo clothing cluster has relied on the capital accumulation and technological improvement of the TVEs, which grew up in the 1980s. The successful restructuring of SOEs and collective enterprises in 1990s contributed to the rapid development of clustered firms and the formation of the industrial cluster. Both of the commodity trading markets (Yiwu China Commodities City and Zhejiang China Textile City) are listed companies with the interwoven ownership dominated by the local government. According to the case study evidence, it was the fuzzy property rights that partly nurtured the initial entrepreneurship, which was crucial to the formation of the textile and clothing clusters.

The research also emphasizes that it has not been the ownership and property rights *per se* that mattered to the rapid growth of textile and clothing firms in the industrial clusters, but the functional ownership and property rights that could be realized through the management of socio-political equity under the precise contextual circumstances of China in transition.

8.1.2. *Institutional entrepreneurship*

Institutional entrepreneurship means "the ways in which individuals or organizations create and develop new institutional norms and rules that redefine appropriate social behavior" (Child *et al.*, 2007, p. 1013). All of the three case studies in the research have demonstrated that the local government acts as an active institutional entrepreneur in the course of development of textile and clothing clusters in China. Since the economic reform started in 1978, the central government has delegated more power to the local government (Zhou, 2012). Although the drafting and adoption of main economic policies remain top-down, the implementation of these policy initiatives is highly dependent on the local government. Therefore, the local government has certain space and opportunities to make institutional innovation to meet the needs of local economic development when they carry out the top-down economic policies. The bottom-up institutional innovation influences the decision-making and the adoption of new economic policies by the central government. The interaction between top-down and bottom-up development policies will continue to bring about institutional evolution in the regional development.

8.1.3. *The commodity trading market*

This research argues that the commodity trading market can be regarded as one of the important institutional arrangements that have played a vital role in the development of SME textile and clothing clusters in rural China.

First, the interaction between commodity trading markets and family workshops has contributed to the emergence and growth of textile and clothing clusters in China. The commodity trading market, which has accelerated the rural industrialization process, has been an institutional innovation associated with the commodity circulation system distinguishing industrial clusters in China from those in Italy. The clustered firms in Italy mainly concentrate on production and the products are sold through professional agents. Even if there are physical commodity trading markets, they are mainly located in tourist cities on a small scale with a high division of labor among clustered firms and with the separation of production and sales, performed as they are in Italy by specialized firms. Additionally, the operational costs of retail stores with some scale are high, so the small-scale clustered firms usually do not participate in the establishment of their own marketing networks there (Zhu, 2003).

The prosperity of the commodity trading market in China indicates that industrial clusters are still developing and that the division of labor within the cluster is not complete. The evidence of case studies reveals that Zhejiang province has been renowned for "small merchandise, big markets". The development of commodity trading markets first took place in the province at the beginning of the 1980s. Many township enterprises and family businesses gathered together to push the sales of their products onto the market. In the late 1980s, with the transformation of TVEs, the model was spread to the whole province. The development of the commodity trading market has become a typical outcome of the commodity circulation system in the rural areas of Zhejiang province in a specific historical period, offering reliable distribution channels for family workshops and promoting the rapid growth of local SMEs. Family workshops have also contributed to the prosperity of commodity trading markets since large amounts of commodities supplied by family workshops at low prices have enabled them to gain competitive advantage. They became an integral part of textile and clothing clusters afterwards.

Thus, the case study evidence illustrates that the commodity trading market has played an important part in the formation and growth of textile and clothing clusters in China. For example, Yiwu China Commodity City and Shaoxing China Textile City have been closely connected with the socks cluster in Yiwu City and the textile cluster in Shaoxing City. The trading volumes of these commodity trading markets account for huge shares of total industrial output of the relevant cities or counties where the commodity trading markets are located. Commodity trading markets engage in the wholesaling business, supplying a bridge between thousands of scattered producers, retailers and consumers. They not only streamline the circulation of commodities, but also save time and costs of the producers and retailers in their search for suitable buyers and suppliers of commodities. The upgraded commodity trading markets are usually modern and spacious. The layout of samples is distinctive with lower and higher grades goods clearly distinguished.

Second, the development of textile and clothing clusters has also been associated with the upgrading of commodity trading markets in China. The commodity trading market provides a trading system with relatively lower trading costs. First, it offers a formal marketing channel for a large number of small-scale production firms within the industrial cluster, achieving external economies of scale through collective marketing. Second, it facilitates the reduction of transaction costs. Since the commodity trading market accumulates a lot of information on price, quality, market demand and supply of relevant industries, the clustered firms can organize production rapidly according to the up-to-date market information and feedback from the sales agents. The buyers and sellers, who obtain relatively complete market information at lower information search costs, can conclude transactions within a short time. Third, the fixed marketing booths within the commodity trading market can reduce the opportunism of sales agents and help them to establish implicit contracts based on trust through multiple repetitive transactions, saving transaction costs and reducing the risks of uncertain transactions with the supervision and implementation of contracts. The commodity trading market has driven the rapid growth of clustered firms in terms of capital accumulation (Zheng, 2003).

The commodity trading markets in China, as an important intermediary between manufacturers and retailers, might disappear gradually with the rapid development of information technology. Manufacturers may well leap over the commodity trading markets and contact their potential buyers directly through Business-to-Business (B2B) e-commerce platforms in the long run. However, as an important institutional arrangement, the commodity trading market will not diminish in China in the short run. The widespread use of the internet actually promotes the flow of information and allows the wholesalers to provide the latest market information to their potential clients, creating more business opportunities for the firms in the local industrial clusters. Meanwhile, the large-scale commodity trading markets in China have also set up online trading markets. These B2B e-commerce platforms enable buyers to search for the commodities they are interested in and supply the latest market updates of each commodity. The integration of the physical and digital markets has improved the competitiveness of the commodity trading markets in China (Wang and Ngoasong, 2012).

China's accession to the WTO has altered the landscape of China's commodity trading markets. *Administrative Measures on Foreign Investment in Commercial Areas* issued by the Ministry of Commerce of China in April 2004 lifted the restrictions on foreign wholesale enterprises, including the restrictions on location, quantity, equity ratio as well as market entry thresholds including minimum assets and annual sales (Ministry of Commerce, 2004). A lot of overseas wholesalers are making use of the golden opportunity to enter the Chinese market and increase their exports there while increasing their imports from China to their home markets, leading to the further prosperity of the commodity trading market. Meanwhile, a lot of international organizations including the United Nations have also set up their purchasing centers within the commodity trading markets in China. The rapid growth of commodity trading market will eventually foster the further upgrading of industrial clusters.

8.2. Institutional Change Through Co-Evolution Between the Public and Private Sectors in Economic Transition under Deepering Globalization

The case studies of Ningbo clothing cluster, Shaoxing textile cluster and Yiwu socks cluster demonstrate that the development of industrial clusters is closely related to the formation of industrial network. Social networks play an important part in the formation of industrial networks in rural China. They can be seen as important assets within the Chinese business system.

The development of private economic sector has been closely linked to the reform and restructuring of SOEs in the past three decades and continues to do so. The clothing cluster in Ningbo has developed on the interaction between informal, formal and global institutional changes. Social network played an important part in the establishment and growth of small- and medium-sized clothing firms in rural Ningbo area. The rural entrepreneurs learned advanced clothing-making skills and took advantage of market opportunities from their fellow villagers in Shanghai. They worked together to expand both domestic and international clothing market. The TVEs also contributed to the development of clothing industry in the region and they were transformed into private firms in the ownership reform of 1990s. The agglomeration came into being when more entrepreneurs participated in the clothing industry. The capital accumulation and technological achievements of TVEs and SOEs in the 1980s and early 1990s laid a solid foundation for the formation of the Ningbo clothing cluster and the rapid growth of clothing firms in the cluster (Wang *et al.*, 2007). Both rural enterpreneurs and local government have accelerated institutional innovation and technological progress to intergrate Ningbo clothing cluster into the global value chain since 2000.

This study has also demonstrated that the commodity trading market is an appropriate focal point to observe how local private and public sectors have interacted. In contrast to the commodity trading markets in other developing countries, most of the industrial clusters in Zhejiang province have developed on the domestic and international business networks of commodity trading markets. A large number of important actors have taken part in business there, including producers, wholesalers, buyers, agents and international traders. The formation and development of the socks cluster in Yiwu City is closely related to Yiwu Commodity Trading Market, whose development has been completely dependent upon the activities of the local government. Yiwu Municipal Government has played an important part in the internationalization of the commodity trading market, leading to the upgrading of the local socks cluster through its information diffusion and collective learning mechanisms.

Shaoxing textile cluster is another case study closely related to the commodity trading market known as Zhejiang China Textile City, which was previously state-owned yet listed on Shanghai Stock Exchange in 1997. The case study has shown that the failure of overall privatization of Zhejiang China Textile City indicates that a commodity trading market cannot always achieve successful outcomes without the active support of the local government. The support of the local government is of great significance to the development of industrial clusters. Subsequently, Shaoxing Municipal Government made substantial investment to renovate and expand the commodity trading market in 2006, regaining its controlling shares. Meanwhile, the clustered firms in the textile cluster of Shaoxing City faced many administrative thresholds in the course of moving from labor-intensive downstream industries to capital-intensive upstream industry. Some clustered private firms have started to produce the upstream materials such as PTA after forming strategic alliances with the SOEs. The case studies indicate that the expansion of clustered firms partly depends on the alliances with SOEs to move towards upstream of industrial sector to gain the market entry and utilize the capital market.

The cases studies in the book have demonstrated that the three types of economic regimes discussed in Chapter 1 — the neo-classical state, the developmental state and the corporatist state — have coexisted at the local government in recent times. For example, the clustered firms experienced a developmental local state because all of the local governments in the three cases make blueprints for industrial development and exercise rights to decide on the use of land for industrial as opposed to commercial or residential purposes and to allocate certain areas for the construction of industrial parks and commodity trading markets. The leading clustered firms, which are important for the local economic development, can usually enjoy the privileges to land use and lower tax rates. Therefore, the local government has the resources and power to control the local economic development.

Meanwhile, some local governments exhibit the feature of the neo-classical state for the local clustered firms, which experience little public interference in their economic activities. The highest expected returns in the form of taxes and income from land sales are often used as the main criteria for allocating industrial sites amongst competing uses because the local economic performance is highly correlated to the promotion of local government officials. Moreover, other local governments, including the subordinate township government and the city-level municipal government, may well negotiate with certain individuals and groups to include the entrepreneurs or managers of clustered firms over the feasibility of establishing and managing firms or commodity trading market over which the local government holds the majority shares. In this case, the local government exhibits the features of a corporatist state.

Therefore, this book would finally like to argue that the theory of local state corporatism or the theory of developmental state alone fails to explain the rapid growth and upgrading of textile and clothing clusters in China in transition. There was a dynamic process of institutional embeddedness, deembeddedness and reembeddedness in the course of cluster development. The above three forms of economic regimes have coexisted and in the past three decades alongside ideological changes at the center associated with the shifts of emphasis implied in the movement from Mao Zedong thought, through Deng Xiaoping's open-door policy, Jiang Zeming's three represents, Hu Jingtao's scientific development to Xi Jinpingi's China dream and adjustments in macroeconomic policies in China implied at each stage. For example, the developmental state paradigm in the 1980s gave way to the local state corporatism (Oi, 1999) in the 1990s. However, with the further development of clustered firms and their adoption of diversification strategies in the new millennium, the governments at various levels have exhibited mixed features of the above three economic regimes with the developmental state paradigm still dominant.

The rapid development of the private sector in China does not necessarily mean the complete retreat of the state. The rapid development of the private sector in China has been and will continue to be critically supported and promoted by the government at different levels. It has been within a framework established by the state that private clustered firms have been given the wherewithal to flourish and become internationally competitive, providing them not only with an appropriate business, legal and ideological framework, but also with crucial public services without which they would have struggled to do so. It is important to see the public sector as a crucial component of any future industrial cluster development. The developmental state orientation at the local level is still remarkable in the course of textile and clothing clusters development and upgrading in China in transition. However, the interaction between the public sector and the private sector has been changing constantly to meet China's contemporary developmental needs in the context of global institutional change and frequent financial turmoils.

The development and upgrading of the textile and clothing clusters in rural China have witnessed extraordinary institutional change through the co-evolution between the public sector and the private sector. The research has added to the literature on SMEs industrial clusters in transitional economies within an institutional approach. The recent research on economic transition has attached much importance to micro-level and macro-level quantitative data with an emphasis on institutional change and economic growth based on the neo-classical growth model. The research at the local level in China has offered a valuable source for identifying new agents of institutional change, their motivations, the dynamic change of SMEs in the textile and clothing clusters and business environment for the rapid cluster development in the rural area of China.

BIBLIOGRAPHY

ADB (2003). *People's Republic of China: The Development of Private Enterprise.* Manila: Asian Development Bank.

Amsden, A (1989). *Asia's Next Giant: South Korea and Late Industrialisation.* Oxford: Oxford University Press.

Arthur, B (1988). Self-reinforcing mechanisms in economics. In *The Economy as an Evolving Complex System*, PW Anderson, KJ Arrow and D Pines (eds.), pp. 9–32. Redwood City: Addison-Wesley.

Bakar, A-HA and BS Begawan (2013). China approves Hengyi's Brunei refinery project. *The Brunei Times*, 27 February. Available at http://www.bt.com.bn/business-national/2013/02/27/china-approves-hengyis-brunei-refinery-project [accessed on 5 June 2013].

Becattini, G (1990). The Marshallian industrial district as a social-economic notion. In *Industrial Districts and Inter-firm Cooperation in Italy*, F Pyke, G Becattini and W Sengenberger (eds.), pp. 37–51. Geneva: International Institute for Labour Studies.

Beckert, J (2010). How do fields change? The interrelations of institutions, network, and cognition in the dynamics of markets. *Organizational Studies*, 31, 605–627.

Bellandi, M and S Lombardi (2012). Specialized markets and Chinese industrial clusters: The experience of Zhejiang Province. *China Economic Review*, 23(3), 626–638.

Blanchard, O and A Shleifer (2001). Federalism with and without political centralization: China Versus Russia. *IMF Stafff Papers*, 48, 171–179.

BP (2009). BP celebrates start-up of Zhuhai PTA #2 plant. BP. Available at http://www.bp.com/genericarticle.do?categoryId=9004958&contentId=7049506 [accessed on 1 August 2009].

Bureau of Fair Trade for Imports and Exports (2006). A collection of cases for fair trade in exports and imports. Beijing: Ministry of Commerce. Available at http://www.gpj.mofcom.gov.cn/accessory/200608/1155778138389.pdf [accessed on 15 September 2006].

Cai, N and J Wu (2008). Social network analysis on denseness of inter-organizational networks in industrial clusters. *Journal of Zhejiang University (Humanities and Social Science)*, 36, 58–65.

Carlo, P (2004). Upgrading and technological regions in industrial clusters in Italy and Taiwan. In *Linking Local and Global Economies: The Ties that Bind*, P Carlo and A Sverrisson (eds.), pp. 170–185. London: Routledge.

CCC Group (2013). Big events of CCC Group in 2012. Zhejiang China Commodity Group Joint-stock Co., Ltd. Available at http://www.cccgroup.com.cn/qydsj/2303.=jhtml [accessed on 18 June 2013].

Chen (2005). UDC makes intensive investment in PTA. Available at http://www.cs.com.cn/ssgs/gsxw/200501/t20050107_574914.html [accessed 15 May 2006].

Chen, J (2000). *The Economic Development of the Areas with High Economic Growth in China*. Shanghai: Shanghai People's Press (in Chinese).

Chen, M (2005). *Asian Management System*, 2nd edn. London: Thomson.

Child, J, L Yuan and T Terence (2007). Institutional entrepreneurship in building an environmental protection system for the People's Republic of China. *Organization Studies*, 28(7), 1013–1034.

China Daily (2008a). Find it in Yiwu. Available at http://www.chinadaily.com.cn/business/2008-06/30/=content_6804216.htm [accessed on 20 April 2010].

China Daily (2008b). Small is beautiful for Yiwu. Available at http.//www.chinadaily.com.cn/business/2008-10/=21/content_7126260.htm [accessed on 20 April 2010].

China Daily (2010). Trade Volume sets new record at China's largest small commodities market. Available at http://www.chinadaily.com.cn/hangzhou/e/2010-01/=04/content_9261008.htm.

China Textile City (2013). An overview of market. Available at http://www.zgqfc.gov.cn/html/marketinfo/aboutqfc.html [accessed on 10 June 2013].

China Textile City Construction and Management Committee (2013). Business promotion preferential policies. Available at http.//www.zgqfc.gov.cn/html/trade policy [asscessed on 17 June 2013].

China Textile Industrial Association (2002). A study on the competitiveness of textile industry in Zhejiang province.

China Union Holdings Ltd. (2004). China Union Holdings Ltd. 2003 Annual report. Available at http://www.china.com.cn/chinese/ch-2004 nrb/sh/pdf/14004382.pdf [accessed on 18 November 2006].

China Union Holdings Ltd. (2009). China Union Holdings Ltd. 2008 Annual report. Available at http://q.stock.=sohu.com/cn/gg/112/612/11261238.shtml [accessed on 1 November 2012].

CHINT (2013). CHINT at a glance. Available at http://en.chint.com/about/?classid=144960712517615616 [accessed on 21 February 2013].

Chow, G (1997). Challenges of China's economic system for economic theory. *American Economic Review*, 87(2), 321–327.

CNTAC (2005). *Overview on China's Textile Industrial Bases and Cities (Towns) with Special Features.* Beijing: China Textile Press.

CNTAC (2007a). *2006 Annual Report on Social Responsibility for China Textile and Apparel Industry.* Beijing: China Textile Press.

CNTAC (2007b). *China Textile Industry Development Report 2006/2007.* Beijing: China Textile Press.

Coase, R (1937). The nature of the firm. *Economica*, 4(16), 386–405.

Coase, R (1960). The problem of social cost. *Journal of Law and Economics*, 3(1), 1–44.

Commons, J (1934). *Institutional Economics — Its Place in Political Economy.* New York: Macmillan.

Cooke, P and K Morgan (1998). *The Associational Economy: Firms, Regions and Innovation.* Oxford: Oxford University Press.

Delixi Group (2013). About Delixi. Available at http://www.delixi.com/english/aboutdlx/aboutdlx.htm [accessed on 7 March 2013].

Department of Commerce of Zhejiang Province (2011). The development of textile industry in China in the past ten years. Available at http://zhejiang.mofcom.gov.cn/article/sjgongzuocly/201108/20110807701957.shtml [accessed on 17 August 2012].

Department of Commerce of Zhejiang Province (2012). A briefing on the main economic indicators of provincial-level economic development zones in Zhejiang Province. Available at http.//www.zcom.gov.cn/zcom/aitz/kfa/kfadt/=7318199.shtml [accessed on 20 August 2012].

Ding, K (2006). Distribution system of China's industrial clusters: Case study of Yiwu China commodity city. IDE-JETRO, Discussion Paper No.75.

Dijk, M and Q Wang (2005). Cluster governance in an emerging city-wide ICT cluster in Nanjing, China. In *Clusters Facing Competition: The*

Importance of External Linkages, E Giuliani, R Rabellotti and M Dijk (eds.), pp. 215–231. Aldershot: Ashgate.

Edquist, C and B Johnson (1997). Institutions and organizations in systems of innovation. In *Systems of Innovaion: Technologies, Institutions and Organizations*, C Edquist (ed.), pp. 41–63. Abingdon: Routledge.

EU (2008). Q&A on the double checking of surveillance system of imports of some textiles from China. European Union. Available at http://trade.ec.europa.eu/doclib/docs/2008/may/tradoc_138820. pdf [accessed on 2 May 2010].

Evans, P (1995). *Embedded Autonomy: States and Industrial Transformation.* Princeton: Princeton University Press.

Fang, M *et al.* (2000). *The Institutional Change and Development Path in Zhejiang Province.* Hangzhou: Zhejiang People's Press (in Chinese).

Fu, X, J Zhang and W Zhang (2009). A comparative analysis of typical high-tech industrial clusters between China and the United States: The case of Zhongguancun and Silicon Valley. *Industrial Technology and Economy*, 28(2), 38–40.

Gabriel (Zhejiang Gabriel Group) (2007). About Gabriel. Available at http://www.china-gabriel.com [accessed on 24 February 2007].

Gambarotto, F and S Solari (2005). How do local institutions contribute to fostering competitiveness of industrial clusters? The upgrading process in the Italian eyewear system. In *Clusters Facing Competition: The Importance of External*, E Giuliani, R Rabellotti and MPV Dijk (eds.), pp. 177–194. England: Ashgate Publishing Limited.

Gao, B and Q Feng (2008). State building and market building: The rise of the largest small commodity market in the world. Paper presented at the annual meeting of the American Sociological Association Annual Meeting, Sheraton Boston and the Boston Marriott Copley Place, Boston, MA. Available at http://citation.allacademic.com/meta/p241629_index.html [accessed on 6 May 2013].

Gao, S (2007). One piece of red thread and one piece of red flag — the socialism with Chinese characteristics leading China (17 October 2007). *China Youth Daily*, p. 4.

Garnaut, R, L Song, Y Yao and X Wang (2012). *Private Enterprise in China.* Canberra. ANUE Press.

Garofoli, G (1991). *Modelli Locali di Sviluppo.* Milan: Franco Angeli.

Giuliani, E, C Pietrobelli and R Rabellotti (2005a). *Clusters Facing Competition: The Importance of External Linkages.* Aldershot: Ashgate.

Giuliani, E, C Pietrobelli and R Rabellotti (2005b). Upgrading in global value chains: Lessons from Latin America clusters. *World Development*, 33(4), 549–573.

Guerrieri, P and C Pietrobelli (2001). Models of industrial clusters evolution and changes in technological regimes. In *The Global Challenge to Industrial Districts: Small and Medium-Sized Enterprises in Italy and Taiwan*, P Guerrieri, S Iammarino and C Pietrobelli (eds.), pp. 11–33. Cheltemham and Northampton: Edward Elgar.

Guerrieri, P and S Iammarino (2001). The dynamics of Italian industrial districts: Towards a renewal of competitiveness? In *The Global Challenge to Industrial Districts: Small and Medium-Sized Enterprises in Italy and Taiwan*, P Guerrieri, S Iammarino and C Pietrobelli (eds.), pp. 35–62. Cheltemham and Northampton: Edward Elgar.

Hakansson, H and J Johanson (1993). The networks as a governance structure: Interfirm cooperation beyond markets and hierarchies. In *The Embedded Firm: The Social-Economics of Industrial Network*, G Grabher (ed.), pp. 35–51. London: Routledge.

He, M (2009). Welcoming address. Available at http://yiwu.gov.cn/ywwwb/english/e_zf/e_hyc/ [accessed on 13 September 2009].

He, P (2005). *The Path to Develop a City*. Beijing: Economic Management Press.

He, Z, L Rayman-Baacchus and Y Wu (2011). Self-organization of industrial clustering in a transition economy: A Proposed framework and case study evidence from China. *Research Policy*, 40(9), 1280–1294.

Hengyi Group (2012). About Hengyi. Available at http://www.hengyi.com/en/company.asp [accessed on 11 march 2011].

Hengyi Petrochemical Co., Ltd. (2012). Hengyi Petrochemical Co., Ltd. 2012 Half yearly report. Available at http://www.hengyishihua.com/upload/pic-Files/2012.11.19_15.56.39_1616.pdf [accessed on 5 June 2013].

Hongmei Garment Company (2013). About Hongmei. Available at http://www.nbhongmei.com/=about.asp [accessed on 4 June 2013].

Hsu, J (2004). The evolving institutional embedd-edness of a late-industrial district in Taiwan. *Tijdschrift voor Economische en Sociale Geografie (Journal of Economic and Social Geography)*, 95, 218–232.

Hsu, J (2010). Towards a late-industrial district. The Construction of learning networks in Hsinchu-Taipei Corridor, Taiwan. In *East Asia: A Critical Geography Perspective*, WS Tang and F Mizuoka (eds.), pp. 89–110. Tokyo: Kokon Shoin Publishers.

Hu, J (2007). Hold high the great banner of socialism with Chinese characteristics and strive for new victories in building a moderately prosperous society in all respects. *The China Daily.* Available at http://www.chinadaily.com.cn/china/2007-10/25/content_6226673.htm [accessed on 5 December 2007].

Hualian Sunshine (Zhejiang Hualian Sunshine Petro-Chemical Co., Ltd.) (2006). About the company. Available at http.//www.sunshine-pec.com [accessed on 1 August 2006].

Huang, M (2005). *The Development Report of Non-State owned Enterprises in China, No. 1.* Beijing: Social Sciences Academic.

Huang, Y and W Di (2004). A take of two provinces. The institutional environment and foreign ownership in China. MIT Sloan Working Paper No. 4482-04, Marsachusetts Institute of Technology.

Humphrey, J and S Humphrey (2002). How does insertion in global value chains affect upgrading in industrial clusters? *Regional Studies,* 36(9), 1017–1027.

Jacobs, G, FD Belschak and B Krug (2004). Social Capital in China: The meaning of Guanxi in Chinese business. In *China's Rational Enterpreneurs. The Development of the New Private Business Sector,* B Krug (ed.), pp. 166–188. London: Routledge Curzon.

Jia and Sun (2004). Langsha and Nengolali awarded famous brands in China. 3 September. Available at http://www.ywnews.cn/system/2004/09/03/=000026497.shtml [accessed on 16 March 2007].

Jin, XR, XW Zhu, ZY You and S Zhang (2007). The industrial clusters in Yiwu and Huangyan District. Available at http://www.ide.go.jp/English/Publish/Download/Jrp/pdf/144_2.pdf [accessed on 28 July 2010].

Jinggong Holding Group (2006). The development process. Available at http://www.jgsteel/group.com/cn/default.aspx [accessed on 28 August 2006].

JSDOFTEC (2006). Measures on the administration of the fund to support companies to 'Go Global'. Department of Foreign Trade and Economic Cooperation, Jiangsu Province, China. Available at http://www.jsdoftec.gov.cn/site/zhongxiaoqiye/NewsDetail.asp?NewsID=7304 [accessed on 12 August 2008].

Karaev, A, SL Koh and LT Szamosi (2007). The cluster approach and SME Competitiveness: A review. *Journal of Manufacturing Techology Management,* 18, 818–835.

Ke, D (2006). Distribution system of China's industrial clusters: Case study of Yiwu China Commodity City, IDE-JETRO. Discussion Paper No.75.

Ke, D (2012). *Market Platforms, Industrial Clusters and Small Business Dynamics*. Cheltenham, UK: Edward Elgar.

KPMG (2009). China: Changes to restricted and prohibited catalogues for processing trade. Available at http://www.us.kpmg.com/microsite/tnf-asiapacific/2009/=TNAP09_09china.html [accessed on 15 May 2013].

Kim, J (2005). The formation of clustering of direct foreign investment and its role of inter-firm networks in China: Case study of Qingdao development zones. In *Industrial Clusters and Inter-firm Networks*, K Charlie, J Borje and R Roger (eds.), pp. 1390–1413. Cheltenham: Edward Elgar.

Kim, J and L Zhang (2008). Formation of foreign direct investment clustering — A new path to local economic development? The case of Qingdao. *Regional Studies*, 42(2), 265–280.

Krug, B and H Hendrischke (2008). Framing China: Transformation and institutional change through co-evolution. *Management and Organization Review*, 4(1), 81–108.

Krug, B and J Mehta (2004). Entrepreneurship by alliance. In *China's Rational Entrepreneurs. The Development of the New Private Business Sector*, B Krug (ed.), pp. 50–71. London: Routledge Curzon.

Kuran, T (2010). *The Long Divergence: How Islamic Law Held Back the Middle East*. Princeton: Princeton University Press.

Langsha (2008). Sichuan Langsha Holding Ltd. 2007 Annual report. *Shanghai Securities News*, 27 February. Available at http://q.stock.sohu.com/cn/gg/111/515/11151547.shtml [accessed on 31 October 2008].

Langsha (2009). Langsha was listed at Shanghai Stock Exchange successfully. 2 June 2009. Available at http://=www.langsha.com/about/news/zqxw/t758.html.

Li & Fung Research Centre (2006a). Overview of Industrial Clusters in China, No. 1. Available at http://www.disgroup.com/profile/pdf/industry_series/LFIndustrial1.pdf [accessed on 20 December 2007].

Li & Fung Research Centre (2006b). Textile and Clothing Clusters in China, No. 5. Available at http://www.disgroup.com/profile/pdf/industry_series/LFIndustrial5.pdf [accessed on 20 December 2007].

Li, F, Y Miao and Z Wang (2010).TonghuaYiwu Trade and Business City has opened. [online] Available at http://www.jlsina.com/news/2010-01-27/90266.shtml [accessed on 10 July 2010].

Li, G, T Zhou and W Du (2013). How to maintain first mover advantage of specialized markets in Zhejiang province. *Workers' Daily*, 10 April, p. 5.

Available at http.//www.zjaic.gov.cn/zjaic/jrgs/yqic/201304/t20130412_
113929.htm.

Li, H (2006). Boundaryless enterprises, innovation of network organisation and
cluster governance. In *The Fifth International Conference on Industrial
Clustering and Regional Development, Beijing, 2006.* Beijing: Peking
University (in Chinese).

Li, H, L Meng and J Zhang (2006). Why do entrepreneurs enter politics?
Evidence from China. *Economic Inquiry*, 44 (3), 559–578.

Li, L (2007). The development record of Zhejiang Yi Sheng Petrochemical
Company Limited. Available at http://wjmj.=bl.gov.cn/news_read.
php?id=32081 [accessed on 18 April 2008].

Li, LN (2009). *Research on the Upgrade of Competitive Advantage of Investment
Promotion in Hangzhou Economic and Technological Development Area
(HEDA).* MPA. Nottingham: Nottingham Trent University.

Li, Y (2004). The private investment in Zhejiang Province faces the license barrier. *21st Century Economic Report*, 20 July. Available at http://finance.sina.
com.cn/roll/20040720/1431883869.shtml [accessed on 15 November 2006].

Li, Y (2009). Hualian Sunshine revives after restructuring. *Xinhua Net*. Available at
http://news.xinhuanet.com/fortune//2009-12/17/content_12661753.htm
[accessed on 30 November 2012].

Libaers, D and M Meyer (2011). Highly innovative small technology firms,
Industrial Clusters, and firm internationalization. *Research Policy*, 40(10),
1426–1437.

Lin, JY (1989). Inhibition of factor markets, institutional reform and induced
technological choice in Chinese agriculture: Theory and empirical evidence.
UCLA Economics Working Papers 575, UCLA Department of Economics.
Available at http://www.econ.ucla.edu/workingpapers/wp575.pdf [accessed
on 30 August 2005].

Liu (2012). Youngor Group: Segment markets, strengthen main business.
Economic Daily, 30 March, p. 9.

Liu, SY (2006). Young or Group initiates to establish the world's largest clothing
making alliance. *Economic Information*, 28 January. Available at http://
news.=xinhuanet.com/employment/2006-01/28/content_4111081.htm
[accessed on 16 May 2007].

Liu, S and D Song (2006). From path dependence to path creation: Path transition
theory and empirical studies of clusters. In *The Fifth International Conference*

on Industrial Clustering and Regional Development, Beijing. Beijing: Peking University (in Chinese).

Lu, L, X Bai and Z Wang (2003). *Exchange of the Feathers of Roosters with Sugar to International Business*. Hangzhou: Zhejiang People Press (in Chinese).

Lu, S and B Ganne (2009). Understanding Zhejiang industrial Clusters: Questions and re-evaluations. In *Asian Industrial Clusters, Global Competitiveness and New Policy Initiatives*, B Ganne and Y Lecler (eds.), pp. 239–266. Singapore: World Scientific Publishing Co. Pte, Ltd.

Luo, F (2011). Rescue yangxunqiao. *Qianjiang Evening News*, 12 April, p. B0001.

Luo, H (2011). Hualian Sunshine revives and the sales of Yuan Dong Petro-Chemical hit RMB16 billion last year. Available at http://zj.people.com.cn/GB/14224567.html [accessed on 5 December 2012].

Markusen, A (1996a). Sticky places in slippery space: A typology of industrial districts. *Economic Geography*, 72(3), 293–313.

Markusen, A (1996b). Big Firms, long arms, circle shoulder: The 'hub-and-spoke' industrial district in the seattle region. *Regional Studies*, 30(7), 651–666.

Marshall, A (1891). *Principles of Economics*, 2nd edn. London: Macmillan.

Marukawa, T (2009). The emergence of industrial clusters in wenzhou, China. In *Asian Industrial Clusters, Global Competitiveness and New Policy Initiatives*, B Ganne and Y Lecler (eds.), pp. 213–238. Singapore: World Scientific Publishing Co. pte, Ltd.

Martin, R and P Sunley (2003). Deconstructing Clusters: Chaotic concept or Policy Panacea? *Journal of Economic Geography*, 3, 5–35.

Mayer, J (2005). Not totally naked: Textiles and clothing trade in a quota-free environment. *Journal of World Trade*, 39(3), 393–426.

Mei, S, M Nie and Y Huang (2006). Research on knowledge flow about enterprise clusters inserting into global value chain. *Science & Technology Progress and Policy*, 24(12), 201–204.

Mingda Group (2013). About us. Available at http://=www.mingdagroup.com/en-about.html [accessed on 4 June 2013].

Ministry of Commerce (The People's Republic of China) (2004). Measures for administration on foreign investment in commercial fields. Available at http.//english.mofcom.gov.cn/article/policyrelease/internationalpolicy/200705/=20070504715768.html [accessed on 1 February 2008].

Mitchell, WC (1937). *The Blackward Art of Spending Money and Other Essays*. New York: McGraw–Hill.

Monga, C (2011). *Cluster-Based Industrial Parks: A Practical Framework for Action*. Washington, DC: The International Bank for Reconstruction and Development / The World Bank.

Montinola, G, Y Qian and B Weingast (1995). Federalism, Chinese Style: The political bases for economic success. *World Politics*, 48(1), 50–81.

Mortel, E (2002). *An Institutional Approach to Transition Processes*. Farnham: Ashgate.

National Bureau of Statistics of China (1996). *China Statistical Yearbook 1996*. Beijing: China Statistics Press.

National Bureau of Statistics of China (2000). *China Statistical Yearbook*. Beijing: China Statistics Press.

National Bureau of Statistics of China (2004). *China, Statistical Yearbook 2004*. Beijing: China Statistics Press.

National Bureau of Statistics of China (2006). *Statistical Yearbook of China Commodity Exchange Market in 2005*. Beijing: China Statistics Press.

National Bureau of Statistics of China (2011). *China Statistics Yearbook 2011*. Beijing: China Statistics Press.

National Bureau of Statistics of Yiwu (2009). The statistical bulletin of national economy and social development of Yiwu City in 2009. Available at http://tjj.yiwu.gov. cn/tjxx/ywtj/201003/t20100329_259011.html [accessed on 15 April 2010].

National Bureau of Statistics of Yiwu (2010). *Yiwu Statistics Yearbook 2009*. Beijing: China Statistics Press.

National Bureau of Statistics of Yiwu (2013). The statistical bulletin of national economy and social and development in Yiwu in 2012. Available and http://tjj.=yiwu.gov.cn/tjxx/ywtj/201 306/t 20130613_481400.html [accessed on 20 June 2013].

National Textile & Clothing Council (2007). *China's Textile Industry Clusters Development Report*. Beijing: China Textiles Press.

Naughton, B (2007). *The Chinese Economy: Transitions and Growth*. Cambridge: The MIT Press.

NBEC (2005). An investigation report on the reform and development of VEKEN Group. Ningbo Economic Commission. Available at http://www.nbec.gov. cn/newsBrowes/zhengCe/detail.jsp?id=725&colFatherId=4 [accessed on 23 June 2008].

Ningbo Municipal People's Government (2013). Overview. Available at http:// english.ningbo.gov.cn/col/col55/ [accessed on 18 March 2013].

Ningbo Municipal Statistical Bureau (2012). Statistical bulletin on National Economy and Social Development in Ningbo City in 2011. Available at http://www.nbstats.gov.cn/read/read.aspx?id=27016 [accessed on 13 November 2012].

Ningbo Yinzhou District Science and Technology Bureau (2008). Ningbo Yinzhou District Science and Technology Report. Available at http://zfxxon-byzogov.xn/govdiropen/jcms_files/jcms1/web6/site/attach/0/100819175=803149.doc [accessed on 18 January 2009].

North, D (1981). *Structural and Change in Economic History*. New York: Norton.

North, D (1990). *Institutions, Institutional Change and Economic Performance*. Cambridge: Cambridge University Press.

OECD (2005). *OECD Economic Surveys: China*. Paris: OECD.

Oi, J (1999). *Rural China Takes Off: Institutional Foundations of Economic Reform*. London: University of California Press.

OTEXA (2013). China textile safeguard. Office of Textiles and Apparel, Department of Commerce, the United States. Available at http://=web.ita.doc.gov/tacgi/eamain.nsf/d511529a12d016de85257393005738 ob15895f5014f25487428525739400560015 [accessed on 3 June 2013].

Parris, K (1993). Local initiative and national reform. The Wenzhou model of development. *China Quarterly*, 134, 242–263.

Perry, M (2005). *Business Clusters: An International Perspective*. Oxon: Routledge.

Pietrobelli, C (2004). Upgrading and technological regions in industrial clusters in Italy and Taiwan. In *Linking Local and Global Economies: The Ties that Bind*, C Pietrobelli and A Sverrisson (eds.), pp. 133–160. London: Routledge.

Piore, M and C Sabel (1984). *The Second Industrial Divide*. New York: Basic Books Inc.

Porter, M (1990). *The Competitive Advantage of Nations*. New York: Free Press.

Porter, M (1998). Clusters and the new economics of competition. *Harvard Business Review*, 76(6), 77–90.

Porter, M (2000). Location, competition and economic development. Local clusters in a global economy. *Economic Development Quarterly*, 14(1), 15–20.

Powell (1990). Neither market nor hierarchy: Network forms of organisation. *Research in Organisation Behaviour*, 12(3), 295–336.

Powell, W and P Dimaggio (eds.) (1991). *The New Institutionalism in Organisational Analysis*. London: University of Chicago.

Qian, M (1999). *Garments in Ningbo*. Beijing: China Textile Press (in Chinese).

Qian, T and J Shi (2008). Taizhou model. Institutional innovation and the development of private economy. *China & World Economy*, 3, 106–119.

Qian, Y (2000). The institutional foundation of China's market transition. In *Annual World Bank Conference on Development Economics 1999*, B Pleskovic and J Stiglitz (eds.), pp. 377–398. Washington, DC: The World Bank.

Ruan, J, J Xiong and J Zhao (2006). The globalization strategy of China Textile City. Available at http://biz.zjol.com.cn/05biz/system/2006/11/17/007993582_01.shtml [accessed on 18 January 2007].

Ruan, J and X Zhang (2009). Finance and cluster-based industrial development in China. *Economic Development and Cultural Change*, 58, 143–164.

Ruttan, V and Y Hayami (1984). Toward a theory of induced institutional change. *Journal of Development Studies*, 20 (4), 203–223.

Schmitter, PC (1974). Still the state of corporatism? In *The New Corporatism: Social-Political Structures in the Iberian World*, FB Pike and DT Strich (eds.), pp. 85–131. Norte Dame: University of Norte Dame Press.

Scott, R (2002). The Changung world of Chinese enterprise: An institutional perspective. In *The Management of Enterprises in the People's Republic of China*, A Tsui and C Lau (eds.), pp. 59–78. Massachusettes, USA: Kluwer Academic Publishers.

Shahid, Y, N Kaoru and Y Shoichi (2008). *Growing Industrial Clusters in Asia: Serendipity and Science*. Washington, DC: World Bank. Available at https://openknowledge.worldbank.org/handle/10986/6429.License:Creative Commons Attribution cc By 3.0.

Shaoxing City Statistics Bureau (2013). 2012 Statistics bulletin of the national economic and social develop bulletin of the national economic and social development of Shaoxing City. Available at http://www.sxstats.gov.cn/tjgb/2013-05-29/10430.htm [accessed on June 2013].

Shaoxing Municipal Government (2013). About Shaoxing. Available at http://en.sx.gov.cn/col/col4126/index.html [accessed on 10 June 2013].

Shenzhou International Group Holdings Limited (2013). About Shenzhou. Available at http.//www.shenzhouintl.com/en/about.asp [accessed on 4 June 2013].

Shi, J, X Jin, W Luo and W Zhao (2002). *Institutional Change and Economic Development: A Study on Wenzhou Model*. Hangzhou: Zhejiang University Press.

Sonobe, T, D Hu and K Otsuke (2004). From inferior to superior products: An inquiry into the Wenzhou model of industrial development in China. *Journal of Comparative Economics*, 32(3), 542–563.

Suqian Daily (2010). Liu Weigao and Yiwu model duplicated. Available at http://www.ywbb.com/news/show-20701.html [accessed on 24 march 2010].

Tetsushi, S, H Yuki and O Keijiro (2012). Productivity growth and job creation in the development process of industrial clusters. World Bank, Washington, DC. Available at https.//openknowledge.worldbank.org/=handle/10986/12143.

The State Council (2007). Notice of the State Council on the implementation of the transitional preferential policies in respect of enterprise income tax. The State Council of the People's Republic of China. Available at http://www.lawinfochina.com/display.aspx? lib=law&id=6572&CGid= [accessed on 1 September 2008].

The Youngor Group (2003). The Youngor Group Shareholding Co., Ltd: 2002 Annual Report. Available at http://www.youngor.com/upload/files/200812/200812100817373550000.PDF [accessed on 18 August 2007].

The Youngor Group (2007). The Youngor Group Shareholding Co., Ltd 600177: 2006 Annual Report. Available at http://www.youngor.com/upload/files/200812/200812100809494432759.PDF [accessed on 25 August 2007].

The Youngor Group (2008). The Youngor Group Shareholding Co., Ltd 600177: 2007 Annual Report. Available at http://www.youngor.com/upload/files/200812/200812091552271542298.PDF [accessed on 11 November 2008].

The Youngor Group (2009). The Youngor Group Shareholding Co., Ltd 600177: 2008 Annual Report. Available at http://www.youngor.com/upload/files/200904/200904161228067881500.PDF [accessed on 15 July 2009].

The Youngor Group (2010). The Youngor Group Shareholding Co., Ltd 600177: 2009 Annual Report. Available at http://www.youngor.com/upload/files/201305/20130503102742237700.PDF [accessed on 18 September 2011].

The Youngor Group (2011). The Youngor Group Shareholding Co., Ltd 600177: 2010 Annual Report. Available at http://www.youngor.com/upload/files/201104/201104200851525043326.PDF [accessed on 10 December 2011].

The Youngor Group (2012). 2011 Annual Report 1979-2011 YoungorGroup Co., Ltd. Available at http://www.youngor.com/upload/files/201204/201204111708298415495.PDF [accessed on 28 November 2012].

UDC Group (2006). PTA Phase II Put into trial production successfully and Hualian Sunshine becomes the largest PTA production base in domestic China. Available at http.//www.udcgroup.com/zh/news/gnnews/205.aspx [accessed on 4 February 2007].

UDC Group (2007). The announcement of No.17 meeting of the fifth board of directors by Hualian Konggu Shareholding Co., Ltd. Available at http://

www.udcgroup.com/manage/doc/upload/20070322095609.pdf [accessed on 1 May 2007].

UNIDO (2000). *Promoting Enterprise through Networked Regional Development.* Vienna: UNIDO Publication.

Veblen, TB (1898). Why is economics not an evolutionary science? *Quarterly Journal of Economics*, 12, 373–397.

Wade, R (1990). *Governing the Market: Economic Theory and the Role of Government in East Asian Industrialization.* New Jersey: Princeton University Press.

Wang, C (2008). *Linkages and Clustering: Key Factors Cultivating Industrial Competitiveness in Host Countries.* Beijing: Economic Science Press.

Wang, J (2010). The innovation of SMEs and development of industrial clusters in China. In *the Rise of Technological Power in the South*, X Fu and L Soete (eds.), pp. 186–203. Hampshire: Palgrave macmillan.

Wang, J (2011). Social networks, innovation and development of industrial clusters in China. In *Sustainable Reform and Development in Post-Olympic China*, SJ Yao, B Wu, S Morgan and D Sutherland (eds.), pp. 97–107. London: Routledge.

Wang, JC (2000). The development prospects for Zhejiang industrial districts from the perspective of Italian industrial districts. *Zhejiang Economy*, 7, 10–12.

Wang, J and M Ngoasong (2012). The internationalization process of Chinese SMEs: Does globalizing wholesale markets play a role? *Strategic Change*, 21(2), 143–157.

Wang, JM, XG Yao and JB Wu (2009). The expansion of textile and clothing firms of China to Asian Least Developed Countries: The case of Cambodia. Asia Pacific Research and Training Network on Trade Working Paper Series, No. 60.

Wang, J and J Wang (1998). An analysis of new-tech agglomeration in Beijing: A new industrial district in the making? *Environment and Planning A*, 30(4), 681–701.

Wang, J, Y Chen and R Sanders (2007). The dynamics of industrial clusters in China: The case of Ningbo clothing. In *China's Globalising Economy — Achieving Harmony, Sustaining Growth*, R Sanders and Y Chen (eds.), pp. 170–184. London: Routledge.

Wang, W (2006). Technological innovation of clustered firms, network embeddedness and cluster upgrading in the Chinese manufacturing industry. In *The*

Fifth International Conference on Industrial Clustering and Regional Development. Beijing: Peking University (in Chinese).

Wang, X (2009). A study on the inter-regional expansion of firms and the upgrading of industrial clusters through the perspectives of network. *Science & Technology Progress and Policy*, 24(12), 52–55.

Wang, Z (2008). *The Private Sector and China's Market Development*. Cambridge: Wood head Publishing.

Wang, Z and J Shi (2006). The growth of China's private sector: A case study of Zhejiang province. *China and the World Economy*, 14(3), 109–120.

Wei, J (2005). EU safeguard measures on textiles opposed. *China Daily*. Available at http.//www.chinadaily.com.cn/english/doc/2005-05/30/content 446793.htm [accessed on 18 July 2009].

Wei, H, Z Shen and M Wang (2002). Structural adjustment: Creating a new textile industry. In *China's Transition to a Global Economy*, M Webber, M Wang and Y Zhu (eds.), pp. 191–204. New York: Palgrave Macmillan.

Wei, Y (2000). *Regional Development in China: States, Globalization and Inequality*. London: Routledge.

Wei, Y (2002). Beyond the sunan model. *Environment and Planning A*, 34, 1725–1747.

Wei, Y, W Li and C Wang (2007). Restructuring industrial districts, scaling-up regional development: A study of the Wenzhou model, China. *Economic Geography*, 83(4), 421–444.

Wei, Y, Y Lu and W Chen (2009). Globalizing regional development in Sunan, China: Does Suzhou Industrial Park fit a Neo-Marshallian district model? *Regional Studies*, 43(3), 409–427.

Williamson, O (1985). *The Economic Institutions of Capitalism*. New York: Free Press.

World Bank (1993). *The East Asian Miracle: Economic Growth and Public Policy*. Oxford: Oxford University Press.

WTO (2001). Agreement on Textile and Clothing. Notification under Article 2.8 (b) and 2.11. European Community. Document G/TMB/N/363/Add.1,16 February. World Trade Organization, Geneva.

WTO (2007). *International Trade Statistics 2007*. [online] Geneva: World Trade Organization. Available at http://www.wto.org/english/res_e/statis_e/iits2007_e/section 2_e/ii58.xls [accessed on 15 June 2008].

WTO (2008). *Trade Policy Review: China*. Geneva: World Trade Organization.

WTO (2011). *International Trade Statistics 2011*. [online] Available at http://www.wto.org/english/res_e/statis_e/its2008_e/section2_e/ii69.xls [accessed on 24 August 2012].

Wu, J and B Guo (2010). Co-evolution of corporate adaptive behavior, networking and industrial clusters. *Management World*, 2, 141–155.

Xiao, LH, YS Han and GS Dong (2006). An analysis of driving forces of vertical integration strategy of youngor Group. Available at http://www.gdpx.com.cn/news/200622043.shtm [accessed on 16 April 2007].

Xie, G (1997). Trace the rise of the small commodity market. In *Small Commodities, Large Markets*, The Historical Documents Office of the Political Consultant Committee of Zhejiang Province (eds.), pp. 1–21. Hangzhou: Zhejiang People's Press.

Xinhua News (2006). Relevant listed companies benefit from obtaining the international pricing right on PTA futures, Xinhua News Agency Beijing. Available at http://cs.xinhuanet.com/qhsc/04/200612/t20061225_1030561.htm [accessed on 2 June 2007].

Xinhua News (2008). Chinese textile giant acquires US garment firm. Available at http://www.china.org.cn/business/2008-01/17/content_1239727.htm [accessed on 1 August 2009].

Xinhua News (2011). China's overseas economic and trade zones: The experimental field of Chinese firms' going global. Available at http://www.mofcom.gov.cn/article/difang/guangxi/201112/20111207867954.shtml [accessed on 3 June 2013].

Xinhua News (2012). Zambia–China trade zone generates $500 m in tax revenue. Available at http://=www.chinadaily.com.cn/bizchina/2012-02/04/content_14537589.htm [accessed on 3 June 2013].

Xu, SQ, J Xu, K Li, B Zheng and Y Zhang (2012). An investigation report on the hi-technology development report in Yinzhou District. Available at http://gtog.ningbo.gov.cn/art/2012/10/12/art_16690_951900. html [accessed on 17 November 2012].

Xu, Y (2006). Not only attraction': Assessing the corporate growth in yiwu city from the development of Lanshan Group. 16 November. Available at http://politics.people.com.cn/GB/8198/74175/74178/5050574.html [accessed on 15 December 2006).

Yan, L (2008). Country report on China's participation in Greater Mekong Subregion Cooperation. *People's Daily*, 28 March 2008, p. 3.

Yang, R (1993). On the supply of institutions. *Economic Research Journal*, 28(8), 45–51 (in Chinese).

Yang, R (1998). The three-phase theory of institutional change in China — On the institutional innovation behaviour of local government. *Economic Research Journal*, 33(1), 3–10 (in Chinese).

Yang, C (2007). Divergent hybrid capitalisms in China: Hong Kong and Taiwanese electronics clusters in Dorigguan. *Economic Geography*, 83, 395–420.

Yang, C and H Liao (2010). Industrial agglomeration of Hong Kong and Taiwanese manufacturing investment in China: A town-level analysis in Dongguan. *Annals of Regional Science*, 45, 487–517.

Yang, K (2012). The dependency of privacy entrepreneurs on the Chinese State. *Strategic Change*, 21(2), 107–118.

Ying, HG, PY Fang, J Liang, XQ Yuan and YQ Mao (2007). Stick to the power of classics: An investigation of Progen influence. *China Business Times*, 3 December. Available at http://business.sohu.com/20071203/n2537=65590. shtml [accessed on 3 June 2008].

Yiwu Commercial News (2008). 30 important events since Yiwu's reform and opening-up in the past 30 years. Available at http://www.yw.gov.cn/zwb/zwgk/ztbd/csjy/200812/t20081230_165112.html [accessed on 23 September 2009].

Yiwu Municipal Government (2012). The sales turn over of Yiwu hosiery industry hit RMB12.5 billion last year. 14 May. Available at http://www.yw.gov.cn/sub/25577/hyts/20120514_410784.html [accessed on 18 June 2013].

Yiwu Municipal Government (2013). Digital Yiwu: An Overview of national economy and Social development in Yiwu city in 2012. Available at http://www.yiwu.gov.in/glb /ywgl/ [accessed on 19 June 2013].

Youngor Group (2013). Historical timeline of Youngor Group. Available at http.//www.youngor.com/about.do?action=dsj&cid=200811180345087595 [accessed on 4 June 2013].

Yutaka, Y (2011). Industrial clusters and micro and small enterprises in Africa: From survival to growth. World Bank. Available at https://openknowledge.worldbank.org/handle/10986/2546 License: cc By 3.0 Unported.

Zeng, G and Y Si (2008). Study on the financial services cluster in lujiazui district of Shanghai. *Area Research and Development*, 27(3), 39–44.

ZFTECB (Zhejiang Foreign Trade and Economic Cooperation Bureau) (2007). Measures on the administration of the fund to support companies to the

Global. [online] Available at http://www.zjjmwo=gov.cn/zcfg/zjzc/2007/11/ 27/2007112700076.html [accessed on 18 July 2008].

Zhang, G, Q Xu and X Liu (2011). Knowledge diffusion within the Datang Sock Manufacturing Cluster in China. *Regional Stuides*, 45(7), 977–996.

Zhang, H (2003). An analysis of present situation, characteristics and competitiveness of textile industry in Zhejiang province. Available at http://www.stats.gov.cn/tjfx/ ztfx/decjbdwpc/t20030909_107243.htm [accessed on 18 June 2008] (in Chinese).

Zhang, H (2006). *The Transition and Upgrading of Local Industrial Clusters on Global Value Chain*. Beijing: Economic Science Press (in Chinese).

Zhang, H (2009). Reverse breakout: Advantages and disadvantages of vertical integration. 21st Century Economic Report, 4 February. Available at http:// www.youngor.com/news.do?action=detail&cid=200811190204542569&id= 200812100=919236854 [accessed on 11 March 2010].

Zhang, W (eds.) (1993). A Study on Yiwu Commodity Market — The Practice of the Socialist Market Economy in Yiwu. Beijing: Qunyan Press (in Chinese).

Zhao, Y (2004). 60% PTA relies on imports and the private investment in Zhejiang Province faces the licensing barrier. 21st Century Economic Report, 18 July. Available at http://finance.sina.com.cn/b/20040718/1513877534.shtml [accessed on 25 February 2006].

Zheng, Y, Y Yuan and C Lin (2003). *Interpreting a "Market Province": A Study of Specialised Markets in Zhejiang Province*. Hangzhou: Zhejiang People's Press.

Zhejiang China Light & Textile Industrial City Group Co., Ltd. (2002–2006). *The Annual Report in the Year 2002–2006*. Available at http://www.zjctc.com.cn/ china/news/dqbg [accessed on 18 September 2007].

Zhejiang China Light & Textile Industrial City Group Co., Ltd. (2004). *The Annual Report in the Year 2004*. Available at http://www.zjctc.com.cn/china/ news/dqbg/2003215_105.html [accessed on 26 August 2008].

Zhejiang China Light & Textile Industrial City Group Co., Ltd. (2006). *The Annual Report in the Year 2006*. Available at http://www.zjctc.com.cn/china/ news/dqbg/2006215_105.html [accessed on 15 September 2007].

Zhejiang China Light & Textile Industrial City Group Co., Ltd. (2006–2011). *The Annual Report in the Year 2006–2011*. Available at http://www.cninfo.com. cn/finalpage/2008-04-18/38890989.PDF [accessed on 18 September 2012].

Zhejiang Entrepreneurs (2009). Grasp the soul of Yiwu model. [online] Available At http://www.zjsr.com/org/listOrgArticle!info.action?entityId=356&articl eId=17541 [accessed on 16 April 2010].

Zhejiang Foreign Trade and Economic Cooperation Bureau (2007). Measures on the Administration of the Fund to Support Companies to 'Go Global'. Available at http://www.zjjmw.gov.cn/zcfg/zjzc/2007/11/27/2007112700076. shtml [accessed on 18 July 2008].

Zhejiang Prospect Industrial Group Limited (2007). About us. Available at http://www.zhejiang prospect.com/En/help.asp?action=about [accessed on 26 March 2007].

Zhejiang Provincial Bureau of Statistics (2011). A study of three industrial belts in Zhejiang province. Available at http://www.zj.stats.gov.cn/art/2011/1/26/art_281_44136.html [accessed on 15 November 2012].

Zhejiang Provincial Bureau of Statistics (2012a). *Zhejiang Statistical Yearbook.* Beijing: China Statistics Press.

Zhejiang Provincial Bureau of Statistcs (2012b). The challenges and solutions to the development of private economy in Zhejiang Province. Available at http://www.zj.stats.gov.cn/art/2011/1/26/art_281_44136.html [accessed on 15 November 2012].

Zhejiang Provincial Bureau of Statistics (2012c). The commodity trading market with transaction volume over RMB100 million have witnessed a stable development in Zhejiang province. Available at http://www.zj.stats.gov.cn/art/2011/1/26/art_281_44136.html.

Zheng, Y (2000). Specialized markets. In *A Study of Zhejiang Modernization Path (1978-1998),* J Shi and W Luo (eds.), pp. 131–162.Hangzhou: Zhejiang People's Press.

Zhong, W (2009). Yiwu Wu Weirong: Yiwu model at the crossroad. Available at http://www.zj.xinhuanet.com/newscenter/2009-03/10/content_15914828. htm [accessed on 22 April 2010].

Zhou, Y (2000). The evolutionary interpretation of institutional change in China. *Economic Research Journal,* 35(5), 3–11 (in Chinese).

Zhou, Y, Y Sun, Y wei and G Lin (2011). De-centering 'spatial fix' — patterns of territorialization and regional technological dynamism of ICT hubs in China. *Journal of Economic Geography,* 11 (1), 119–150.

Zhou, W (2009). Bank financing in China's private sector: The Payoffs of political capital. *World Development,* 37(4),787–799.

Zhou, W (2011). Regional deregulation and entrepreneurial growth in China's transition economy. *Entrepreneurship & Regional Development. An International Journal*, 23(9–10), 853–876.

Zhou, W (2012). Regulatory models and entrepreneurial growth: Evidence from China's transition economy. *Strategic Change*, 21(2), 119–142.

Zhu, H (2003). *Industrial Clusters in Zhejiang Province*. Hangzhou: Zhejiang University Press (in Chinese).

Zhu, H and W Gai (2001). An empirical research on industrial flexible agglomeration and regional competitiveness. *Economic Theory and Economic Management*, 11(5), 70–74 (in Chinese).

Zhu, X, J Tang and Y Xu (2008). The role of human factors in the development of industrial clusters — A Case study of the textile industry in Shaoxing, Zhejiang Province. *Reform and Strategy*, 24(1), 115–117.

INDEX